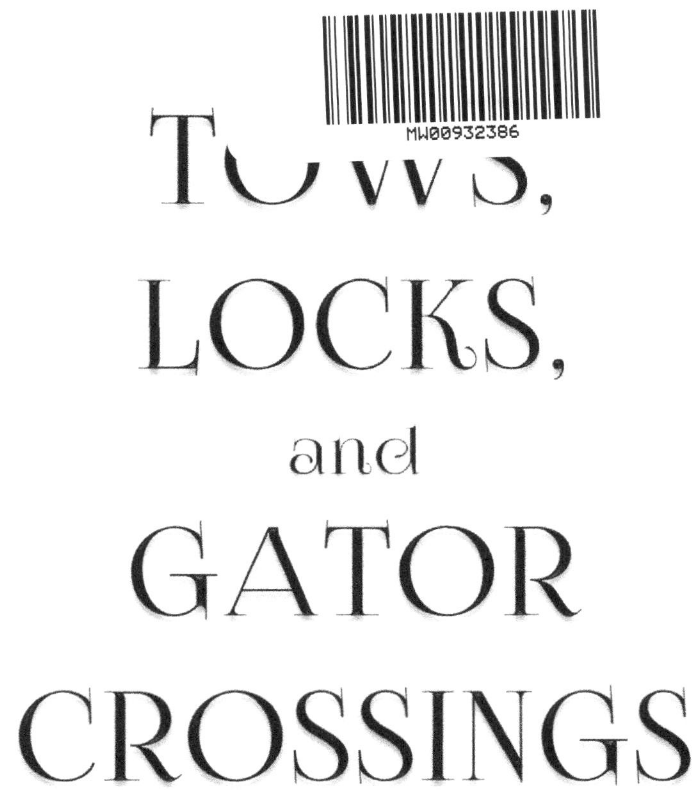

TOWS, LOCKS, and GATOR CROSSINGS

Stories and Experiences of a Mississippi River Boat Captain

HENRY E. ELLIOTT

Tows, Locks, and Gator Crossings

ISBN-13:978-1514243510
ISBN-10:1514243512
Also available in eBook

Cover photo: Henry Elliott
Cover Design: Elizabeth E. Little, Hyliian Graphics,
www.hyliian.deviantart.com
Interior Design: The Author's Mentor,
www.LittleRoniPublishers.com
Photographs property and copyright: Henry Elliott
Interior Illustration: Kim Ridley

PUBLISHED IN THE UNITED STATES OF AMERICA

A Note from the Editors:

Captain Elliott has a genuine voice that reflects the warm and wonderful culture of the River and its People. The editors of this book have worked diligently to help Mr. Elliott only with the more obvious inconsistencies that would distract the average reader from the telling. As often as possible, we have left his voice and tenor the way he intended—like that of a Riverboat Captain.
Enjoy the read!

~ The Editors with The Author's Mentor

A Note from the Author:

This book holds the short stories of my life as a riverboat captain on the Mississippi River and most of its tributaries, The Gulf Intracoastal Waterways, and bayou's flow—about seven thousand miles. In addition, readers will come to understand how river towboats and barges operate. There are more people than I can name that have made this possible. In this industry, you'd never make it on your own; you need a lot of help. I was fortunate enough to have help from many. Most who see that you are trying to help yourself will be willing to help you.

My special thanks to the following people:
My wife, Dianne Elliott
my daughter, Elizabeth Elliott
and my sons, J.W. Fry
and David Fry

1 ST. PAUL MN
2 UPPER MSSISSIPPI RIVER
3 CHICAGO, IL
4 ILLINOIS RIVER
5 MISSOURI RIVER
6 ST. LOUIS, MO
7 CAIRO, IL
8 ALLEGHENY RIVER
9 MONONGAHELA RIVER
10 PITTSBURGH, PA
11 OHIO RIVER
12 GREEN RIVER
13 CUMERLAND RIVER
14 TENNESSEE RIVER
15 NASHVILLE, TN
16 KNOXVILLE, TN
17 WABASH, RIVER
18 TENNESSEE AND TOMBIGBEE WATER WAY
19 MEMPHIS, TN
20 ARKANSAS, RIVER
21 LOWER MISSISSIPPI RIVER
22 YAZZO, RIVER
23 VICKSBURG, MS

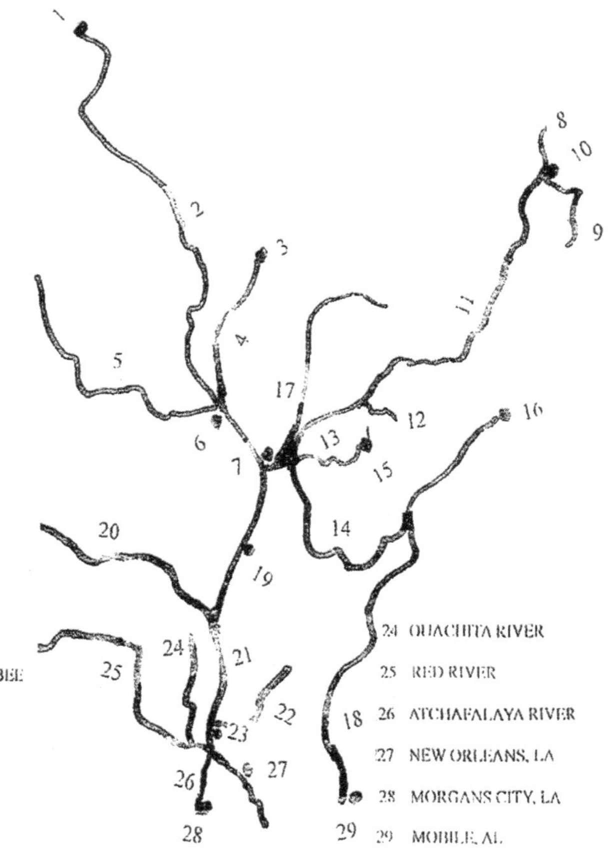

Table of Contents

List of Tows, Locks, and Gator Crossings

Stories and Experiences of a Mississippi River Boat Captain

by Henry E Elliott

As a Pilot, or Captain, I've run on the following bayous, bays, canals, and rivers:

- Atchafalaya and Old River -From Mississippi River to twenty miles below Morgan's City, LA
- Allegheny River-From Pittsburgh to Springdale Pa.
- Arkansas River -From Mississippi River to Little Rock, AR
- Brazos River -From Gulf Intracoastal Waterways to about fifteen miles to pick up a dredge
- Big Sandy River -From Ohio River to Ashland Oil dock
- Colorado River (TX) -From the Gulf Intracoastal Waterways about fifteen miles to deliver a dredge
- Calcasieu River -From the sea Buoy to Koppers & US Steel
- Cumberland River -From Ohio River to Nashville, TN.
- Chocolate Bayou -From Gulf Intracoastal Waterways to Chemical Plant
- Corpus Christi Ship Channel-From ICWW to Corpus Harbor
- Green River -From Ohio River to about thirty miles to swap boat tows
- Galveston Bay and Trinity River- From Houston ship channel to Sulfur mine below Liberty, TX

- Gulf of Mexico -From Venice La to Port Arthur, TX
- Harlingen Channel- From Gulf Intracoastal Waterways to Port of Harlingen
- Houston Ship Channel and Buffalo Bayou – From Sea buoy to just below main street, Houston
- Illinois River, Chicago Canal, Through Chicago lock across Lake Michigan to Gary, IN
- Gulf Intracoastal Waterways – From Brownsville to Pensacola, FL
- Kanawha River- From Ohio River to Charleston, WA
- Mermentau River-From Gulf Intracoastal Waterways to Jennings, LA
- Missouri River-From The Mississippi River to somewhere between St. Joseph and Kansas City, MO
- Morgan's City to Plaquemine, LA, Locks the land side route
- Morgan's City to Plaquemine through Bayou Sorrell locks
- The Mississippi River's two parts: the lower Mississippi, from the gulf of Mexico to Cairo, Illinois
- The Upper Mississippi from Cairo, Illinois to St Paul, MN
- Monongahela River- From Pittsburgh to Newell, PA
- Neches River- From Gulf Intracoastal Waterways to about Twenty Miles above Beaumont, TX
- Ohio River- From Cairo, IL to Pittsburgh, PA
- Ouachita River-From Red River to Sterlington, LA
- Port Allen & Morgan's City Route-From Port Allen to Morgan's City, LA
- Red River – From Old River to just below Alexander, LA

- Sabine River- From Gulf Intracoastal Waterways to about twenty miles above Orange, TX
- Tennessee River-From Ohio River to above Knoxville, TN
- Tombigbee River-from Mobile to Demopolis, AL
- San Bernard River-From Gulf Intracoastal Waterways to Sweeny, TX
- San Jacinto River from- From Houston Ship for about fifteen miles
- Vermillion River- From Gulf Intracoastal Waterways, just as far as I could go to protect my barges and boat from a Hurricane
- Victoria channel-From Gulf Intracoastal Waterways to sand and gravel pit and the port of Victoria

Introduction

After leaving military service, I went to work on the boats. I'd only been working on the boats a few days, when I saw the largest riverboat I'd ever seen. It was coming into Houston, Texas, and the barges trailing behind made the rig look as if it was a mile long.

I told another deckhand, "I'd like to work on a boat like that." But making up that many barges gave me second thoughts. He only had a regular unit boat oil tow—four or five oil barges. I wanted to get on that barge and look around, but I never got the chance. I'd seen big ships before, but never a boat pushing that many barges.

You don't travel all that fast on water. One time we went down the river when the water was high—the fastest I'd ever gone south on the Mississippi. We averaged seventeen miles an hour with an empty four-piece unit boat tow from Cairo, Illinois, to the Old River—the Mississippi River—which was about seventy-five miles above Baton Rouge. The slowest had an average of about three miles an hour from Baton Rouge to Cairo.

Of all the many companies I've worked for, I've only filled out, at most, six applications. I only had to look for a job one time, because the work always came to me. If you were honest, dependable, and did a good job you never had a problem getting, or keeping work. There were always problems that you had no control over and you'd make mistakes that were no one's fault but your own. You had to take the blame, forget it, and move on.

While lying in bed in 1973, recovering from back surgery, I spent a lot of time going over my life. What a mess. I made notes of my experiences as they came to mind. I tried to document things in order, but to no avail. The experiences merged as one. For instance, I worked on one particular boat three separate times over approximately eleven years. I remembered things that happened on the boat, but I could not recall the correct sequence of events. There have been a number of boats that I've worked on more than one once. I've worked for a company that operated nine boats and I've worked on them all at one time or another. I've worked on seven different boats in a thirty-four day period.

In 2002, I was working in an office with a lady and we began talking. She asked me questions about my life and working on boats. She said, "You should write about your life."

"Who would care to read about my life?" I asked.

"Your children," she answered.

"I've made too many mistakes for me to put them down for my children."

"Your children may learn from your mistakes."

She mentioned this to my wife. I gathered all the notes I'd made and began reviewing my life experiences. I've gone over my life *thousands of times* in the last forty years. I've written most of what I remembered and continue to remember more and more.

My wife wanted me to write only about my boating experiences. I'm going to try and do this, but some of it still will not be in the order that it happened—dabbed with jokes, pranks, and real-life stories. There are things about working on a boat that the everyday person won't understand.

I hope to clear the waters with this book.

The author, Henry Elliott

1. Moving the River and Barges

Most of the River towboats have one steering rudder behind the propeller. There are two rudders in front of each propeller for steering while backing up.

A *double-locking boat tow* is when you are too long to lock and you lock it in halves—you get your first part in the lock then separate it from the second part. You back the second half out so that the crew can lock and pull the first half. When they get the first out you then go in with the second half. When the second half is locked to the level of the first half you put the two halves back together. Then you are on your way.

The most common types of boat tows are unit boat tows and barge line boat tows. Unit boat-tows, in most cases, move oil. These barges are fifty to fifty-four feet wide and vary in length, but are commonly from one hundred twenty feet long to about two hundred ninety-seven feet long. The length depends on how many barges you have. Most barges are twelve hundred feet or less.

I went north one time with four fifty-two feet by two hundred ninety-five feet barges, plus a one hundred fifty-foot barge, then the boat. With a tow that long and narrow you have to be careful, or you'll break it in two. Sometimes two unit boat-tows are placed side-by-side—if you have the horsepower; this is only for northbound boat tows. When coming southbound with empty barges you shorten your boat-tow up with a wider width.

A barge line boat tow is made up of many barges—thirty-five feet wide and one hundred ninety-five or two hundred feet long. When I retired, the boats you drove south, were five barges long and up to seven barges wide. I do know that boat-tows have gotten larger since I left. When you start north—in most cases—your barges are empty, but they may have loads.

When you narrow the width of the boat tow the length increases. The longest I've ever gone north was with approximately seventeen hundred sixty feet, including the boat. We were eight barges long and five barges wide—thirty-eight empties and two loads. There are mixed boat tows with all size barges. I had a boat tow with eight barges and I don't think there were any two barges the same size.

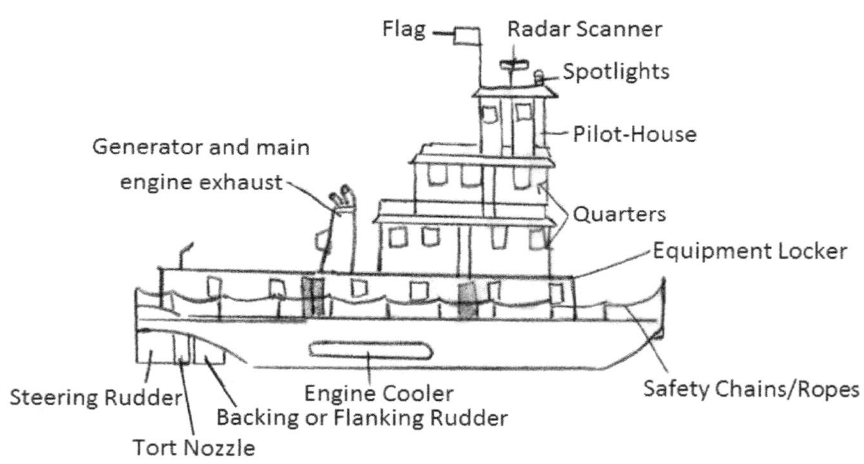

BOAT

This is a mix of oil and cargo barges that hauls grain, coal, salt, iron ore and a lot of other things.

Double unit oil tow. It can run as a single unit tow width and length 108 x 1030 feet plus the boat.

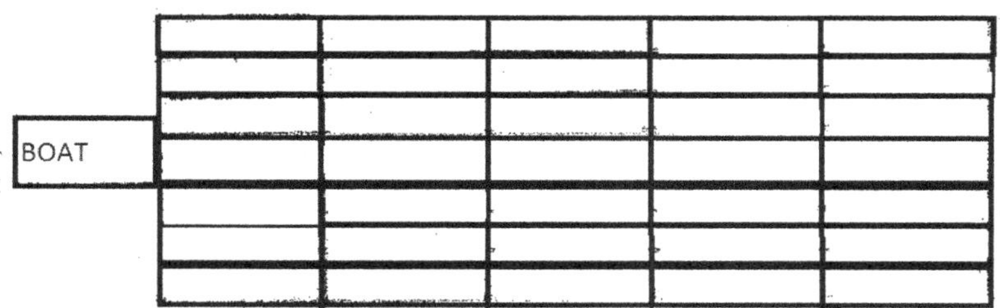

This is a regular barge line town on the lower Mississippi River. Boat and tow is 245 feet wide, 1200 feet long. Barge is approx. 5 acres of barges (35 barges.)

2. Live and Learn

WINO LOGIC

I begin in 1944 and '45, during World War II when there were no men to work on the boats. I was twelve, or thirteen, working on the boat with Cotton, my eldest brother (his real name is Ervin). Most of the available help were *winos*. One of the regular deckhands my brother hired was a drunk named, Archie. We were walking to the boat one day when we saw Archie leaning on a post with pencil and paper. Cotton asked, "Wha cha doing Archie?"

"I don't ever get any mail, so, I'm writing myself a letter."

"What does it say?" my brother asked.

Archie responded, "How do I know? I won't get it 'til tomorrow."

QUICK STUDY

I left the military at 3:30 PM on December 22nd, 1952 from Ellington AFB in Houston. I went straight to work and ate supper on the boat in Sweeny, Texas. I knew most of the general rules. You didn't sit in the Captain's place at the table. If you griped about the cook's cooking, you cooked the next three meals. If you knew the engineer needed help, you went and helped him without being told. If you broke a line you spliced an eye (loop) in the line. If you were told to do something and it wasn't done, the Captain asked, "did you forget?" The third time he asked, "you packed your bags?" This didn't happen very often. We didn't have welfare then.

Once, I fouled a line and it broke. (I couldn't get it loose or take it off.) I told the Captain I didn't know how to splice a line. I was shown *only once* how it was done.

***

The crew arrived in Houston. While our barges were being pumped off, I went to the dock office. The Captain ordered a six-hundred feet coil of two-inch diameter rope. I had to cut the coil of rope into seventy-foot lines and splice an eye in each end. When I finished, the Captain asked, "Do you know how to put an eye in a line?"

"Yes." I thought that was the end of it. It wasn't. Our barges were pumped off and we went back to get another load of oil.

While the barges were being loaded the Captain asked, "Do you know how to splice two lines together?"

I said, "No."

He found pieces of line for me to splice together. He showed me *one time*. That was all I needed and I was good to go.

Later, the Captain asked, "Do you know how to splice cable?"

I said, "No."

He ordered a twelve-hundred foot roll of one-inch cable. He gave me the length each cable needed to be including the eye (some of these were for other company boats). The Captain showed me twice how to splice an eye in the cable. With the first couple of eyes I almost wore the cable out trying to get the eye right. During my first fourteen days I learned how to splice an eye in rope and cable, as well as splice rope together. I learned fast. The other deckhands cleaned and did whatever else was needed, but they weren't allowed to help me. When there wasn't anything on deck to do I was sent to the engine room to help.

After the preparing lines, cable, and working in the engine room, I spent my six hours plus on the barges with the tankerman learning to load and pump barges. You had to do this for six months before you could take the test for a tankerman's license. It took me two days to take the test. There were so many "what if" questions. A lot of the answers had to be written out and some were long.

***

When I first went to work on the boats, we didn't have regular glasses to drink from, so we drank from tin cans. Sometimes we'd get the engineer to solder a handle on the drinking cans. On one boat there was a captain that brought a glass from home. I can't remember the first boat that had regular drinking glasses.

We had an old man for a cook. We had a new mate getting on the boat while we were at the dock. The cook and I were sitting in the galley when this man came in and introduced himself. The cook welcomed him on the boat and invited him to make himself at home. Jokingly, the new mate said, "I sleep with the cook at home."

This made the old man mad. "I'll tell you one thing—you mess with me and you won't ever sleep with your wife again," and the cook walked out.

The new man said, "I was just picking at him."

About a minute later the cook came back with a .45 Colt. "This says you had better stay on your grounds. No hard feelings, just so we understand each other."

After that, they got to know each other and got along good.

BROTHERS

I had two older brothers. I didn't like working for them because they didn't know when to stop working me. Both of my brothers were captains. I was complaining to the mate how my brother worked me and I was going to quit. The mate had been a captain running the rivers for years—he wanted a change so he went back to the river. It made him mad when I said what I did.

He said, "You stupid little idiot. Don't you know what your brother is doing? He's trying to teach you the right way to do things. He wants you to see how everything is done and they're right."

Lesson learned.

***

My oldest brother and I hauled sand out of the San Jacinto River to Houston. We slept while they were loading the barge. We worked four days on and four days off. The boat was a wooden hull boat with a GM (General Motors) six-seventy-one as main power.

When we arrived in Houston they didn't have our barge unloaded so we went to the dock office. The bunks were in the back of the pilot-house and my brother had the bottom bunk.

He woke me up and asked, "Would you like to get wet? You had better crawl out the front window because we've sunk."

This little boat sank so deep they needed a crane to pick it up. They had another engine ready. Our drinking water was in a five-gallon stainless steel tank. Our generator for light ran off the main engine. The only oil we needed was for the main engine and it was in a five-gallon can.

This all took place about midnight. They picked the boat up, put another board on the bottom and put it back in the water. There were four bolts that bolted the smoke stack, four bolts to hole the engine, and four bolts for tail shaft. At 8:00

AM we were on our way after our barge in Houston. When we came back by the dock office, our relief was there and we got off.

We didn't use cable and ratchets to hold the barges together when we had more than one barge. We used what they called *grass rope* to put between the barges. We would take the boat and pull the lines as tight as we could. We had a two-inch pump at the coupling. We would wet those lines down and they'd be tight. The boat really didn't have much power, but if the line got loose we'd wet them down and they'd be tight. I don't think either of us ever went back on that boat.

***

I remember working with my brother on our way to Corpus pulling two barges. A norther broke out as we crossed Matagorda Bay. Our boat-tow line broke and the barges went into the gulf. My brother called the office at Port O'Connor, Texas. They wanted to know what he was doing on a land phone line.

"I just wanted you all to know that I am renting a plane to go look for our barges because they've gone to the gulf." They hired a boat in the gulf to bring the barges to us.

***

There was a man at the dock who was a ventriloquist. I found out he could do this, and I decided to have a little fun. My brother was loading a barge. I went up on the dock when my brother was looking down in the loading hatch.

I said, "Tell him to get his head out of that hatch."

My brother stood up and looked all around. He didn't see anything so he started looking down again.

This man said, "I said get your head out of that hatch."

The fourth time my brother stood up and looked all

around. There was no place for anyone to hide anywhere near where my brother was except up on the dock. My brother started easing back to the boat. As soon as my brother got out of sight I made a run for the boat. When I got on the boat I saw a deckhand who said your brother is looking for you.

When he found me he said, "Will you go out there and load the barge so I can get ready to get off? I was looking down in the hatch and a voice said, 'get your head out of that hatch.' It is time for you to get off. Will you go load the barge and see if you hear anything?"

I went and loaded the barge. It was over thirty years later when I told him about what I had done. That long, it still didn't go over very well with him.

LEARNING

I'd been working on the boats about forty-five days. We were coming from New Orleans towing empty barges. I walked into the pilot-house and told the Captain (not my brother) that I had no intentions of decking the rest of my life.

He looked at me and said, "I'm not going to give you anything." He cursed a few words during his lecture. "You will have to earn it," he continued. "Now drive."

He stood there a few minutes and watched me. He then went outside and sat down in front of the pilot-house where he could see what I was doing. This was on my off watch. I learned to steer, dock, make locks and make bridges, very little on company time.

***

Ninety-five percent of what I learned about handling a boat I learned on my off watch. I'd gone to work on the boats in December and the following August we were coming through the Brazos River Flood Gates, near Freeport, Texas, when the mate had to get off. I told the Captain if he would help me at the Galveston Causeway, we could take the boat tow to Houston. He said, "Do you think you can stand a pilot-house watch?

"Of course," I said.

When I made it to the Galveston Causeway I didn't need his help, but he was there just in case. I let the Captain sleep until we got to Houston—about nine hours. When we got to the docks he let me dock the barges. He corrected me if I was doing something wrong. This was before a license was required.

The Captain told our personnel man what I'd done standing the afterwatch from Brazos River to Houston, plus docking the barge. The personnel man told the Captain he wanted me to work in the engine room for a while. I already knew what all the bells and whistles stood for. I'd already worked in the engine room a little bit. You don't want to get your bells and whistles mixed up and that was easy to do when an engineer had to answer as many bells and whistles as I rang and blew.

If a captain needed extra power, he would blow four whistles. (Two fast, a pause a second, then two more.) The engineer would give the captain everything the old engine could stand. When the captain wanted to go back to regular speed he would blow one whistle.

I worked in the engine room for about a month. The boat was engine room control, which meant you had to let the engineer know the direction and speed you wanted to go, before you could go. It was hot and a lot of work. When I got out of the engine room, there was an old captain that was willing to take me on in the pilot-house.

I never had any real problems, no accidents until I reached a point when "I knew it all." I got *mile-happy*. Another man who worked for the company took me to the company shop and he cussed me more than he talked. He told me the company didn't expect me to make as many miles as the Captains. "They don't want their barges or boats in the shipyard because you are *mile-happy* and you don't know what you're doing," he yelled.

I was a different pilot-house person from that day on. I made as many miles as I could safely and didn't worry about how many miles I'd made. I didn't care how many miles the other pilot, or captain, made either. I did what I could and if the company wasn't satisfied with that they could let me know. My kids wanted me home anyway.

***

I got a job I thought would be a dream of a lifetime—a 1400-horsepower boat and 290 ft long x 50 ft wide barge. Loading in Port Arthur, Texas, and pumping off in St. Louis, Missouri—working two trips on and two trips off. When I got on the boat I found out they'd had six or seven pilots in a year. I couldn't figure out why. When we got out in the river I found out why. The one barge and boat was so wild it was just hard to hold it between the buoys. You could hardly take your eyes off the channel to look at your radar. I lasted two trips, and then I had to go. Barge lining was a lot easier.

IN CHARGE

My first trip up the river as a pilot was on a one barge boat tow. The Captain hadn't ever been above Baton Rouge. I'd been to Greenville, Mississippi one time decking. We got a channel report and a light-list book at Red's Boat Store in Baton Rouge. I didn't even know there was a chart for the lower river. In fact, the first chart I saw of the lower river was in 1961, or 1962. A chart then was useless, because the river changed so much and so fast. You used a channel report and lightlist book. We were above Helena, Arkansas, going up around a point. The captain, or myself—at the time—didn't know the whereabouts of a chute that ran from the river and came out just above Helena harbor.

The captain was running as close to the shore as he could. When he got to the chute, it sucked us down into the chute. We were southbound. I came on watch and had no idea where we'd come out, or even if we would come out in the river. I'd got down where I could see a boat coming up the river. I called him and told him we'd been sucked down the chute (I didn't know what it was then).

He said, "Just hang with it. You'll be back in the river in a minute. When you get back around that point pull out in the river, or you'll be doing this trick again."

I said, "Live and learn."

He said, "Don't feel bad. You're not the first and won't be the last."

After we got to Memphis and unloaded, we came out into the river southbound. There was a boat southbound just ahead of us. We ran about their same speed. I called the pilot and told him I was going to follow him and if he had to slow down to let me know. We followed him all the way to Old River. I followed him, but read my channel report anyway.

The next time I came south, I was on a four-barge loaded boat-tow. I had me a light-list book and a channel report. When I got off watch I would read it over and over. When I came on watch I saw where we were and I would read about the miles I would cover in the next six hours. The port captain stood watch with me.

He said, "I'm not going to say a word to you unless I see you are fixing to mess up."

I ran the Memphis Bridge without a problem. I was off watch when we got to the Greenville Bridge and he woke me up, because he wanted me to run it. I was on watch when we got to the Vicksburg Bridge. This was a different ball game all together. When I lined up to make the bridge he told me what to do.

On this same trip the port captain told me if an owner is on the boat and starts to tell you how to run the boat just get up and give him the controls. Don't ever work for but one person. There is no man that can satisfy two people. I had to do this a few times in my boating career.

One time I started in a lock with the owner on the boat. I was easing up to the lock when the owner came to the pilot-house.

He said, "Captain Henry, it looks like you are going at this all wrong." I just backed away from the control.

"You make the lock and I will be in my room."

He went to hollering, "NO, NO, NO!" and he went downstairs.

When I got the boat tow in the lock I went and found him. I said, "I need to talk to you."

We went to the pilot-house. "I have a few things to say, and then you decide. The port captain hired me to run this boat. Now, if you think your port captain has made a poor decision in hiring me I will be getting off when we get to the terminal."

"Oh no, Henry. That's not about to happen."

"Well, let's get one thing straight then. When I am operating this boat you keep your mouth shut." I figured this would make him mad.

All he said was, "I can handle that." I should have been a little more diplomatic, but I said what came to my mind and it worked.

***

There was a lock on the Upper Mississippi that I hated to make southbound. We had a deckhand that had worked the upper river about twenty years. He was in the pilot-house when I told him I hate to make this lock with a purple passion.

He asked, "Why? I've worked with a number of pilots like you. Most pilots and captains don't want a deckhand to tell them how to do anything."

I said, "If you can, tell me I am one captain that has learned a lot from deckhands."

He said, "If you will do just like I tell you, you won't

have any trouble."

I said. "Shoot, Luke. The gun is loaded." I listened and did just like he told me. That fifteen-barge boat tow just fell in the lock. From that day on I never had any trouble at that lock.

MEDICATING

The Port Captain was on the boat to check me out. We came down on Vicksburg Bridge as he stood behind me. He instructed me to hold the center of the boat tow on that right bridge pier just as long as my nerves could stand it, and then hold it ten seconds longer.

I said, "My nerves are getting thin."

He said, "Boy if your nerves are that thin you will never make it." I knew one thing—he wasn't going to let me hit that bridge. I settled down.

I said, "I'm fixing to let it fall off the pier." When I put the boat on straight rudder and saw how fast it was falling away from the pier, I knew I was in good shape. I turned around and started talking to the Port Captain before we ever cleared the bridge.

He said, "You see what I mean by nerves now, Henry? I'd been out here on the river a few years and seen pilots and captains take everything in the world to help their nerves out. If I find out one of our people that does that he is gone. When you get to where you have got to drink, or take pills for you to do your job, it is time to change jobs."

Over the years, I've worked with a lot of pilots and captains that would take a little white pill when they were coming to a bad place in the river, or a bridge they couldn't make without a little nerve help. I've worked with a pilot that would drink half bottle of Nyquil before making a bridge. I don't know why he didn't go to sleep. It had just enough alcohol to settle his nerves. I worked with a Captain who had six half pints of whiskey in his room.

I said, "Captain, you aren't supposed to have that whiskey on the boat."

He said, "Come in and close the door."

He had a mark halfway on the bottles. He said, "That is for *So-and-So lock* that is for *bridge So-and-So*." I always made sure I was up at one of those places.

REGARDING DEAD BODIES

I was coming down the Allegheny River, when I got on the upper lock wall I look behind the wall. There was a body floating. I told the lock man. He called everybody he was supposed to call. The Coast Guard made us stay there about six hours. I answered so many stupid questions—the men that were asleep when I'd seen the body had to answer questions too. It cost my company a few hours in time lost. I learned a lesson and the company reinforced it. *If you see a body floating keep your mouth shut.*

***

We were westbound in the canal, just west of the Mermentau River in Louisiana and we were in one of the worst lighting storms I'd ever seen. A boat behind us was struck by lightning and one person was killed. It destroyed the engine and burnt up all the electric motors and radio. We dropped our barges to go back and help. They'd already taken away the dead man in the john boat. We helped them tie-off to the bank until their company could send a boat.

***

I was at the mouth of the Cumberland River, at Smithland, Kentucky, waiting on a boat to bring some barges out of the Cumberland River. Four or five of us were setting on the river side of the boat when we saw this big box floating. There was another, but came right beside the boat. They were caskets.

When they flooded Old Eddyville, they missed some graves moving them to higher ground. When the water got over the loose coffins, they floated out of the ground.

CLOSE CALL

I was on one of the fastest boats on the river at the time. We both pushed unit boat tows, which were about 1,150 feet long. Twice we raced from Old River to Cairo, Illinois—approximately 650 miles. The one who was ahead stayed ahead. One of us might try to pass, but the other wasn't about to slow down so he could pass. It was captain against captain and pilot against pilot. We had a fair river condition and I tried for thirty miles to pass him. I could get about half my boat tow up alongside and that was it. There was a southbound barge line boat tow and I had to drop back.

I came out of the upper Mississippi River at Cairo and another fast boat was coming out of the Ohio River. We both had empty barges. He was about a half mile ahead of me. When we got to the Old River, he was about three miles ahead of me. He went on to Baton Rouge and we turned and went down to the Atchafalaya River.

While on this boat, you had to watch it like a hawk northbound. At the speed we were traveling, you didn't want to over, or under steer. If you were running in slack water you didn't want to run your bow barge out in the open current, the current was on the side of the barge, because it was going to break all the cables holding the barges together. You worked your boat tow out into the current so you wouldn't have all the current on the side.

I had a Corps of Engineers contact pilot to get on at Natchez and he was steering the boat. The river was high enough you could take some short cuts. I was sitting on the couch reading when I looked out and he was about to run from slack water into the current where the current was going to hit the bow barge on the side. I told him to kiss that bow barge good-bye and sure enough, the bow and second barge broke all the cables that were holding them together. There was a boat that had his boat tow tied off and he helped us catch the barges and get them back in boat tow. That was a lot of pressure when you break sixteen one-inch cables on each side holding the barges together, plus there was some two-inch rope as safety. There would be four to six rounds of two-inch rope between the barges on each side. The contact pilot never rode a boat with me again. He came to get on another boat and when he found I was on there he didn't get on.

While working on the fast boat I would come out of the Gulf Intracoastal Waterways into the Atchafalaya River northbound below Morgan's City, Louisiana. When we got to the Atchafalaya, we had deep water and I came full ahead. I had my marks to run by and I usually never slowed down northbound for the railroad bridge if it was open.

There were two men on the bow barge. When the steering went out, I started backing as hard as the boat would back, and called the engineer and told him if those engines had anymore RPM give them to me. One of the deckhands said, "You are stopped."

I ask how close I was to the bridge.

He said, "I can step off on the bridge."

As the old saying goes this stopped me from sucking eggs at this bridge. From then on I would go slowly until I was lined up to make the bridge, then I would come ahead.

CUSSING

I've worked on over ninety boats that I can name. They might have been my regular boat, or just tripping. I have traveled over 7,000 miles of river, canals, and bayous. On these ninety-plus boats, the horsepower range was from a boat with a 60 horsepower Murphy Engine to 7,500 horse triple screw. I've ran the lower with 4,000 horsepower boats and twenty-five barges and 6,000 horse and twenty-five barges and 7,500 horsepower and twenty-five barges. I've worked on a little harbor tug, larger tugs on the Gulf Intracoastal Waterways, then boat tow boats from 500 horsepower to 7,500 horsepower, plus an off-shore supply boat.

Years ago, I was pilot on this boat with twenty-five barges and a 4,000 horsepower getting in shape to make the Vicksburg Bridge. I had been on the radio checking for northbound traffic below Vicksburg Bridge. No one answered. I shoved the throttles wide open when I saw a northbound boat. The Captain sat on the couch behind me. When I saw the boat I pulled my cap off and stomped it and did a little cussing because he wouldn't answer his radio. If I had known what boat it was I would have known he would be up out of way. It was one of those speed unit boat tows.

When I got down through the bridge the Captain said, "Did all that cussing help any?"

I said, "He got out of the way didn't he?" I'd never heard this man say a curse word.

He said, "Henry, do you know what Shakespeare said about cussing?"

I cursed and said, "I don't care."

He said, "If a person has to curse to express themselves, they are too stupid to express themselves otherwise."

It made me mad at first, but then I got to thinking about it. He was right. I began watching the words I used and still do.

3. Northers, Banks, and Being Henry

CLOSE CALL

In the early fifties, beer was shipped into Houston on barges. We took the beer barge from another boat. A guard came with the barge. They built him a little shack to stay in on the barge. He ate on the boat that had the barge in boat tow. The guard told me he enjoyed the journey, but he wouldn't want to do it again. He said that they left him three days at one place without food or water. He had some canned food, and a little water from another boat that dropped the barge. Back then you had very few fleets. You would tie a barge off, put two lights on the outside corners and forget it. When we docked, guards surrounded the barge. You would have thought we had a barge load of gold.

BOAT TOWS & MARRIAGE

Over the years, I've seen people build some great boat-towing companies and lose everything. I worked for such a person. One day we saw one another at a shipyard after I quit working for him.

He said, "Henry, I'm going to sell all my boats, barges and contracts." He was having marital problems.

I asked, "Why?

"If something happens to me, in six months' time, everything I've worked for would be gone. I'm going to enjoy some of what I worked so hard to build."

He did sell, divorced, and his wife got half of everything. A few years later, another man and I went in a restaurant. The man I was with asked if I knew the woman across from us. She was sitting with another gentleman.

"It seems like I've seen her some where's. That's *Mr. So and So's* ex-wife. She ran through her part of the settlement and I think he said that she was a clerk at Sears. I asked about their boys. They had both been to prison if I'm not mistaken.

Hover craft ice breaker breaking ice on Illinois River

We were crossing Galveston Bay when a norther broke and blew the tide out. About three-hundred yards from where we were, I saw a man waving. The crew put the outboard over the side to go see what he needed. It was a man and a woman.

When the tide went out, their boat was high and dry. I got them on board then called the Coast Guard out of Galveston to come and pick them up. It was all over the evening news.

When we got to our dock office, I saw a crowd of people and I wondered what had happened. The news people asked me all kinds of questions, but I walked by them without answering. A woman stepped in front of me and said, "Are you the captain?"

"Yes," I replied.

I found out right then and there the woman on the boat with the man wasn't his wife. She proceeded to call me every name in the book. She said, "Why didn't you leave him out there to die? At least I would have got insurance money. I can't live with him after this because it's all over the news, and I'm sure I won't be able to get any child support from him."

***

I was working on a stand-by boat in Houma, Louisiana. We were there where they were loading fish oil on a barge. There was four of us. We worked a week on and a week off. We had a phone on the boat. One man's wife would call him on Wednesday night and Saturday night when he was working. He was always talking about how much his wife loved him after these calls. We could receive calls, but we couldn't make long-distance calls. We were playing cards in the galley and this same man would not shut up about his wife's love for him.

I said, "If my wife called me on honky-tonk nights about the same time I would think something fishy was going on."

There was a pay phone about a hundred yards away. This man laid his cards down and went to the pay phone. In a few minutes, he came back mad and in a hurry. He packed his clothes and in five minutes, he was on his way to Port Arthur, Texas. I never saw him again, but I heard he divorced and his wife married his brother.

***

We were pumping a barge off in Houston on a Sunday. The driveshaft between the pump and engine broke. It needed a machine shop to repair the shaft. The captain told me to call the port engineer. I was walking up on the dock to call the Port Engineer, when the owner and his wife drove up. He didn't hear the pump engine running.

He asked, "What's the problem?"

I told him that the driveshaft broke and needed to go to a machine shop. I told him we already had all the pieces together. They were in a brand new Cadillac. The owner told us to go get the shaft and he would take shaft to get it fixed. We had a bunch of rags to lay it on.

The owner's wife said, "You are not going to put that old greasy thing in my car."

The owner said, "That old greasy thing bought this car; put the shaft in the trunk." We did over the objection of the owner's wife. When the owner brought the shaft back he was by himself. When he started to leave he said, "I hope my door key fits when I get home."

***

I was in Chicago where we were pumping black oil. The Port Captain was there and he stayed until we finished pumping. When we finished, he told us that he was going home—he lived in Texas City and had an apartment in New Orleans. He was going home and I was getting off at Memphis.

When I got on the plane in Memphis the Port Captain was sitting by me on the plane—he always had a woman besides his wife.

I said, "I thought you were going home."

"Well, I got sidetracked." I knew what he meant. My wife was to meet me and his wife was to meet him in Houston. Our wives hadn't met before. The Port captain and I were in the Airport when I saw our wives. I could almost see the daggers coming out of his wife's eyes.

He said, "Sweetheart, you just don't know how much trouble I've had getting home to see you. There is so much snow and ice, the planes couldn't land and take off, the buses are not running, no need to rent a car because of the snow and the trains are frozen to the track."

His wife looked at me and said, "Henry, have you ever seen such a big liar in your life?"

A few years later, the same Port Captain and I were working for another company. He was captain on one boat and I was captain on another. Both boats were tied off in Paducah, Kentucky. He had a woman on the boat with him. I stood on the side of one of the boats looking up the hill, when I saw the other captain's wife drive up. I ran upstairs, told him his wife just drove up. "Will you run up town to look for me and tell her where you are going?" he asked in a panic.

I went up the hill and met up with her. I told her that I was going to town to look for her husband.

She said, "I'll go with you, we will stop at the first beer joint that's more than likely where he is."

We made a few stops and then went back to the boat. She drove up on the hill. Her husband stepped out from behind the wall just huffing and puffing like he was *give-out* from running.

He said, "I have been chasing you all for three blocks. He grabbed her for a big hug she pulled a .38 out of her purse, put it to his belly.

"I should shoot you for getting Henry in the on the deal and I should shoot him for doing it for you".

We both got out of this alive.

***

We were northbound in Memphis about 2 AM when a deckhand ran into my room hollering, "Henry, get to the pilot-house quick, the pilot is going crazy."

I jumped out of bed and went to the pilot-house in my shorts. The mate was at the controls and he was just holding still in the water. After a moment, the pilot settled down so that I could talk to him. He was crying and I told him to sit down for a few minutes then maybe he could tell me what the problem was. I took the controls and moved over for a southbound boat tow. I was also holding up to see if I could find out what was wrong. He handed me a letter to read.

I said, "I don't want to read your mail."

"Read it and I think you'll understand."

He had a wife and four children. I read the letter and I told him to go home and take care of his problem there. The children were at his brother's home. There were so many people who ran off with other people. It was hard for me to understand what happened until I read the letter about three or four times. He drove up river two or three times to talk about his problems after he got off.

The pilot's wife ran off with the pilot's father. The pilot's mother ran off with the pilot's wife's father. The pilot's wife's mother ran off with the boat town banker. From what I could find out, this all happened in a twenty-four hour period.

The pilot went home. His brother and his wife didn't have any children, so they took them in. Right then, their mother was willing to sign adoption papers. The pilot signed the papers so his wife couldn't come back to get them. The pilot's brother and sister-in-law adopted the children. The last time I talked with him he had not remarried and was furnishing all the money to raise the children. He said his brother and wife were raising the children right.

***

We were on dry dock at Paducah, Kentucky, and there was ice and snow everywhere. I saw this man coming down the hill in shirtsleeves. He got a deckhand to bring him to the pilot-house where I was. He said that he needed a job and had never worked on a boat before. We were short one deckhand so I hired him. While talking to him I knew he was just no ordinary person that would be looking for a decking job, but I let it go.

I said, "I may never see you again, but I am going to give twenty dollars to go buy a few things. I have a work coat you can use."

He went to town and about an hour, he was back, ready to work. I called the mate to meet the deckhand. When he said he was ready to work, that is what he meant. He worked all time he was on watch and times when he wasn't. He learned fast.

We went on north and when we got back to Memphis, the regular Captain came back and I got off. Before I got off, he told me he would like to ride five or six months. I told the regular Captain. I figured forty-five days he would be ready to get off. When I came back, I was riding pilot because the regular captain was on. I asked the deckhand how he was making out.

He said, "Great." He had been on the boat about thirty days then. He wanted to know if they would hold his checks in the office after the first one until he got off. I had talked to the regular captain about how he wanted to ride if he could. He said that he didn't see any problem. The deckhand had never mentioned any family or anything about his personal life, and I didn't ask. I knew there was something, but I didn't think it was the law.

If the engineer needed help he was there. He mopped the engine room floor when he was off watch. I gave him a nickname and that stuck until he got off. He rode five and half months.

One time, he said, "Henry, I would like to talk to you when you get off watch."

I said, "That will be fine."

He came to my room and he told me the whole nine yards. He had given me a false name and social security number. He was an Electrical Engineer with a number of degrees. He'd been making top dollar and was working in Illinois. When he came home, his door key didn't fit anymore. His wife withdrew eighty-thousand dollars out of the bank, put the farm and home up for sale. She got him fired from his job and every time he got another job she would get him fired somehow.

He got a lawyer, but didn't have any money. The lawyer stopped the sale of the house and farm, but said he had to bring him five thousand dollars. He went to an uncle and borrowed five thousand dollars, which he didn't have to spare.

"That is when I came to you for a job, because I knew my uncle needed his money. That is the reason I gave you a false name and social security number."

He called me a few months later and he had got his house and farm back. The eighty thousand dollars was gone. That was the last I heard from him for a few years.

The boat that he and I had worked on was going up the Ohio River ahead of me. The lock man at lock fifty-two called the other boat and wanted to know if Henry Elliott was on there. They told the lock he was about five miles behind him. The lock man called me and told me who was waiting on me. When I got on the lower lock wall he came and got on. He got the cook and they went to my room, me not knowing. He came on to the pilot-house, he told me the whole story from the time got off up to this date. I was getting off watch so he and I talked until we were ready to leave the lock.

We went on up the river and when we got back to lock fifty-two the dam was down. They said that they had a box there for Henry Elliott. We put our boat over the side to go get the box. I opened the box there was a tailor-made suit, shirts, ties, alligator shoes, socks, and five one hundred dollar bills. I finally got him after about six months to thank him. That was the last time I ever heard from him. When he and the cook went to my room they were getting all my sizes. Everything fit perfect, except that I had to have the pants cut off a little.

JUST BEING HENRY

I was in the pilot-house trying to put a barge behind a dock, under some ship lines that ran from the ship to shore to hold the ship to the dock. I rang bells and whistled to the engineer. Each bell would tell him whether to go ahead, or a stern. The whistle told him what speed I wanted the engine. We tied the barge off and took the boat to the dock. The engineer came up and asked if the boat was tied off good. I affirmed. The engine started ahead then stopped. Then the engine would go astern, and the engine would speed up and slow down. The captain was up and we happened to meet at the engine room door.

The captain asked the engineer what he was doing. "I'm just trying to catch up on all those bells and whistles Henry used trying to get that barge behind the dock."

***

When crossing Galveston Bay in the Houston Ship Channel with one barge, a big ship came up behind us. There was also an out-bound ship. They were going to meet about the time as they passed us. I moved over as far as I could. The ship behind me came to close and we were pulled into his suction. It sucked us up against the ship and we were pulled along for the ride. Our boat stayed alongside for fifteen or twenty miles. This was something that happened often. When the ship pilot was ready for you to get off, he'd put his engine in reverse for just a minute and it would break the suction. I just sat up there and *let the good times roll.*

***

On another occasion I worked on a wooden hull tug which belonged to the same man that owned the little boat that sunk. It had two engines and one propeller shaft. There weren't any reduction gears to connect the two engines together. There were gears and chains, which made the engines turn the propeller shaft.

We were in a bay east of Port Isabell, Texas, in a long straight channel. I got a deckhand to hold the steering wheel for me. I asked, "All you got to do is follow that boat up ahead."

I'd only been downstairs a minute when we started hitting bottom. I took off to the pilot-house. The boat we were following turned off so my deckhand did exactly what I told him to do—follow that boat. We went on up the channel into "no-man's-land" when one of the big chains from an engine to the shaft broke. The chain was too large for us to handle. With the one engine turning the propeller we were barely moving until another boat took our tow.

We went on to Houston with only the boat. I never worked for that man again. Thirty days of working with junk was enough for me. After riding the canal on two wooden-hull boats and a steel-hull boat—a piece of junk I rode for about three or four days— I told him, "I quit."

***

We were on a boat towing two barges in Galveston Bay and a norther (a strong autumn, or winter wind) had blown in. The water was so rough we had to let our boat-tow line out all the way. There was a crew boat running wide open. He didn't see the boat tow line, hit it and turned a complete flip. I really don't think he saw the boat or the barges we were towing. It wasn't funny then, but it still makes me laugh. The four people got banged up pretty good, but they survived. I never figured how it landed right side up.

***

I hired a deckhand in Memphis southbound. He was standing watch with me so every once in a while he'd come by and check on me. He asked me how long I'd been doing this. "All my adult life."

"Have you ever done any other kind of work?" he asked.

"A little," I said. "After you work out here a couple years you get too sorry to do anything else. You begin to see things that aren't there. I had my binoculars looking for an extra tall tree that stood out at night because there was a small town behind the tree, that caused the tree stand out. You see I know there isn't a river light down in that bend, but I can see one."

He asked if he could he use my binoculars and I handed them over. He said, "There isn't a light down there."

"I know it, but I can see one."

He went on downstairs and was telling the crew what I'd said, but I didn't find that out until later.

One of the boys said, "The Captain has been doing this so long, sometimes at night he sees bridges that aren't there. He'll blow his horn thinking he's meeting another boat, plus a few other things."

I had told him that sometimes traveling southbound worked on your nerves. I said, "I know of two men that cracked up and jumped in the river." This was true. This goes on all the way to New Orleans and back just below Memphis. I was about thirty miles below Memphis and I heard him coming up the stairs. I was in a good stretch of river. I pulled my clothes off real fast and stepped outside. It was dark in the pilothouse and I began to think he wasn't going to miss me. He turned his flashlight on and didn't see me and saw my clothes piled up in the floor. Someone hollered, "The Captain has jumped over the side."

I ran back inside, put my clothes on, and everybody showed up. I reached over and turned the pilot-house light on and I ask what the matter was. The engineer said that the deckhand came running down stairs saying I had jumped over the side.

I turn around and looked at the boy, then said, "It usually takes a couple years for the river to start working on you and this is your first trip." He did what I wanted him to do—he quit. He was a good worker, but he had one problem, being away from home. He almost walked off a barge. I asked him what he was thinking. He was thinking about his wife and baby.

If a captain will watch a new hire and listen to him, he'll find out if he needs to go, or stay. If you let him stay when you know he's a hazard to himself and the crew that's bad. I have hired people who I knew would make a good hand if I could get their minds on their job. There have been four people that I've forced off the boat who came back to work for me and later have made good pilots, or engineers. I didn't fire them—they left with a chance to return.

***

I pulled something on my engineer and he didn't say a thing about it. We were coming down river and it was high. The fog rolled in and I got backed in under a point. Every now and then I would almost lose my electric power. Then the main engines would slow down and speed up. Every time this would happen I would have to make some adjustments. I was worried something was going to quit. I called the engineer to the pilot-house to see if he could find out what the problem was. He knew I was in a bad place even under this point. I had to sit right there and watch that boat tow just like I was running wide open. When we changed watches it all stopped. The generators leveled out also the main engines. I figured the engineer was just paying me back.

I worked with this captain when he was making a lock southbound; he did it differently from anybody I ever worked with. Instead of coming down the shore to the lock, he would be out in the river a few hundred feet out. He would stop then flank to the lock guide wall. You could almost bet your paycheck he was going to hit the lock guide wall so hard he was going to break one or more cables. He would get the boat tow flanking, moving sideways so fast and he couldn't do anything about it until it hit the lock guide wall. This captain had been making locks on the Ohio River for at least thirty years. I found out why he did this a little later. At some time he had come down the shore, when he hit the end of a lock wall and sunk a barge, so he wouldn't come down the shore any more.

MORE CLOSE CALLS

In the canal when we towed barges, we took a little six-volt battery and put a light on each barge behind us. On the back barge, we would put one on each back corner. The mate woke me up and said that he couldn't see the back two lights. I told him they probably went out. When we got to Matagorda Bay, we stopped because of the weather. I came on watch and when we saw daylight and I could see we had lost our back barge. There was no place to tie off, but the wind would hold the other barges against the bank while we went back and retrieved the lost barge.

***

One of my cousins worked with me on a boat without an engineer, so I asked him to go down and grease the engine. "What do I grease?" he asked.

I said, "Just squirt a little oil on anything you see moving." This engine was *direct reversible*, which means when you are moving ahead and want to go astern, the engine had to be stopped and started in another direction. This engine had a big fly wheel with a brake. When you pulled the lever up to stop, air pressure forced the brake down on the fly wheel to stop the engine. I got to the barge dock and pulled the lever to stop and the engine just kept running until I hit the bank. I went down and there was oil all over the fly wheel and brake.

I ask my cousin, "Why did you put oil on that brake?"

He said, "You told me to squirt a little oil on anything moving and that thing was gettin' with it."

***

Early in my career, we pulled empty barges behind us and pushed loads in front. It was an art to pull barges and put them exactly where you wanted. I'd been told about the land owners on the San Bernard River. They didn't want a barge to touch their property. From the Intracoastal Waterways to Sweeny was about twenty-five miles. I was like a long-tail cat in a room full of rocking chairs. I'd been told if I heard somebody holler, show myself, and then get behind something, because they were going to shoot the window out of the pilot-house. A man drew me a map of the San Bernard River and the places I could let the barges hit, or land on the bank. My watch was about over and I let the barge drag a man's property. A man hollered and I showed myself then got down. He shot the window out of a door. I only know of one person ever getting shot on the San Bernard River.

***

I was on a boat that had only one engine. We were moving barges from Texas City to Broussard's Fleet on the Mississippi which was about five miles above Plaquemine Locks at Plaquemine, Louisiana. They had not opened the Port Allen—Morgan's City route. There were two routes you could take from Morgan City to Plaquemine. One, you could go up through Morgan's City and through Bayou Sorrel Locks. The other, you would go on the Gulf Intracoastal Waterways past Morgan's City and turn up on what was known as Land Side Route and you would come out just above Bayou Sorrel Lock. About the last ten miles before you got to Plaquemine Locks, you had to put your barges loaded, or empty on a boat-tow line because the Bayou was so crooked you had to start towing the barges behind you, which you didn't have much control over. Plaquemine Locks was just large enough for one barge, 195 foot barge and boat.

We stopped our tow about two miles from Plaquemine Lock. We locked one barge and boat and took the barge to Broussard's landing on the Mississippi. We picked up a barge then lock back through to the canal—one-out and one-in. This usually took over twenty-four hours to lock five barges each way. The boat had one engine, and on our last barge into the river we cleared the lock and hit the current when the engine threw a rod. We drifted for hours before we met someone to put us to the bank and tie-off.

***

We were southbound and needed to go into the shipyard at Greenville, Mississippi. At the time, the channel was across from the entrance to Lake Ferguson near the shipyard. You went down and crossed the river to the lower light of Island eighty-four which sits about a mile below the mouth of Lake Ferguson. We needed to turn around and go up the Mississippi shore. The company sent a boat out to help us turn around and push back up the river to enter Lake Ferguson.

I came on watch before we made it into Lake Ferguson. A sand\bar had built up on the Mississippi shore just at the entrance to the lake. That's where we lost the starboard string of barges. The boat that was helping us was faced up to that string of barges. I backed up to where we could get some ropes to help pull those barges off ground. There wasn't anything unusual about a bar building up there, but they always put a buoy when the bar built up.

We got them off ground and went on into the shipyard. When we came out there was a buoy on the corner of the bar.

MORE WINO ACTION

There was a swing bridge across the San Bernard. Every Saturday afternoon an old drunk man came by about 4:00 PM. When the bridge was open, the arms were down and there were red flashing lights that meant nothing to this old man. He'd run through the barricade, land in river, land on barges, hit the side of boats, and never got hurt except for a broken arm and some scratches.

One Saturday afternoon we were coming out of Sweeny with a loaded boat-tow. It was about 4:00 PM and I was off watch and out on the barges walking around as we were going through the bridge. Here came the old man and the bridge tender told me to run. The old man landed on our barges and it wrecked his car. I ran to the car. The old man was okay and taking another drink of whiskey. All he said was, "Who moved the d%#$ bridge?" They called two winch trucks. When they got there the mate backed in the bridge so the winch trucks could pull the car off the barge.

PROBLEM SOLVING

I was on a little boat that had a direct-reversible 188 horse-powered engine. There was a lever in the pilot-house that would stop and start the engine and give it fuel. I was about to get fuel and I had to head straight into the dock. As I pulled the lever, the engine didn't stop. The boat hit the dock and the front went under a twelve-by-twelve timber and was caught by the head that we run a line around. The galley was in the forward hole. The only way we could get out was pump water in the galley. We put two, or three feet of water in the galley before the boat would come out.

I went down in the engine room to see why the engine didn't stop. The airline that went to the engine brake was broken. I'd used dock water to put in the galley, but I didn't say anything about what had happened. The office got a bill for a few thousand gallons of water. I was called and they wanted to know why I bought that much water. "The water tanks wouldn't hold that much."

I said, "The galley will."

I then told my boss what happened. He said, "I don't know what we are going to do about that line, we can't keep one on there without it breaking ever few months."

I said, "I can fix it if you all want to spend that much money."

He said, "Fix it."

I took the old line off and took it to a high-pressure hose place. I told them I want a high-pressure flexible airline hose that would stand heat and pressure with fittings just like on the old line. Ten years later, I went back in the canal to work a little while and that line was still on the boat.

***

We were westbound at the Brazos River Flood gates and the Brazos River was high. They had a limit of one barge at a time. I had a plan if I could talk them into it. The pilot was up and I got him to put me off on the lock wall. I walked into the lock house and it was full of the big brass from the district office. I started telling them of my plan.

The lock master said, "One barge at a time."

The one that had the braid on his hat and shoulder spoke up, "Will it work?"

"It may not work, but it won't do any damage to either the east or west gate," I said.

"Do you take full responsibility for any damage to either gate?"

"I will," I said without hesitation.

He said, "We got six witnesses to this. Go ahead."

They had a tow waiting and this gave me time to get my mate and explain what I was going to do. "If you lose a barge we both will be out of a job," I told him.

After the other boat locked we eased through the east gate and let the barges fall down river. The mate had put so many ropes between the barges; if *they* went to the gulf, we would go. When I got ready, I told the mate to break the center coupling on the port side. I had told the mate to leave a lot of slack, because the two head barges were going to swing around about forty-five degrees when I started backing in the west gate. I got the boat and first two barges through the gate and the two front barges started lining up. The deck crew was taking up all the slack in the ropes on the port side. I had them put cross ropes between the barges so they would almost be in line when the third barge got to the gate. I didn't get in a hurry and just eased the four barges through the west gate. The deck crew made up the other barges together. I went down a little ways and turned the boat loose and went around to the other end, faced the boat up and we were on our way. We saved about twenty-four hours.

When we came back we had to trip our barges because, what we did with empties would not work with loads. I got a real nice letter from the engineers, which I kept for years. I don't know if anybody else ever tried it again. I did it twice. You got to have a boat that can handle backing up.

Henry Elliott

4. Alligators and Snakes

We were northbound on the Morgan's City Plaquemine Route when the fog rolled in. I put the barge in the trees. I told a deckhand to go out there and get a line out. He came back to the boat and said, "I'm not going out there because everything is covered with water."

I said, "You watch it and *I'll* go get the line."

I went down the ladder. Just as I got to bottom, a bull alligator let out a noise you could hear back to the boat. I didn't need those steps on the ladder to get back upon the barge. We were right across from a little boat dock where a bunch of people stood. I yelled, "Alligator! About two dozen people rush over. Everyone had a light. That alligator never had a chance.

Somewhere between Bayou Sorrel locks and Plaquemine locks the road was right next to the bayou. There was a sign on the road that read "Alligator Crossing." Somebody had turned pointing it more toward the bayou than the highway. I'd seen it before and hadn't thought much about it. A deckhand was in the pilot-house with me when he saw the sign. The deckhand said, "Do you think those alligators read that sign before they cross so they will know where they can cross?"

I said, "Alligators are smart."

***

The Victoria Texas Channel hadn't been completed. We took barges into Seadrift Chemical plant and loaded down to a five-foot draft. Then, we brought them out to Gulf Intracoastal Waterways and pumped into another barge, took the barge back and loaded it down to five feet, brought back to Gulf Intracoastal Waterways, and pumped into the barge and then went back again.

On one of these trips, two of the boys decided they wanted to go swimming. They didn't see the snakes. We didn't know where they came from, but there were about two dozen snakes. When the swimmers got back to the boat those snakes were after them. I think that was the first and only time I ever saw snakes swim after a human being. We could never figure out what kind of snakes they were, by it being salt water. They tried to get on the boat. We poured a little oil around the boat and they left.

***

We were on the on the Gulf Intracoastal Waterways east of Vermillion locks. There was a hurricane out in the gulf. My intentions were to lock through the locks and get where I had a high bank on each side of the canal. This would help stabilize the boat during the storm. The tide had already risen so high the locks had stopped working. When I got to the Vermillion River in Louisiana, we doubled our barges up and I turned and went up Vermillion River as far as I could, so I would have protection to keep the empty barges from going miles from the canal. Still, we had problems—keeping the snakes *of all kinds* off the boat. There were three men going round and round the boat looking for snakes that were trying to get on the boat. When salt water gets in some snakes eyes they just got madder.

***

While waiting on the weather at Matagorda Bay, there was a dredge in the canal. They were pumping mud and water onto Rattlesnake Island. When rattlesnakes started slithering out of their holes, there was one boat that had rope bumpers. They killed several snakes that made it onboard, I think we killed two. Later, everyone thought they saw rattlesnakes and dreamed of them that night.

***

My brother and I were on the same boat about four miles east of Calcasieu Locks, Louisiana, which is south of Lake Charles. My brother was steering and myself and another man were in the pilot-house when two windows shattered. We all hit the floor. We didn't hear the shot, but we knew what it was. We think somebody had a duck blind built on their boat and was back in a wash where we couldn't see them. When we passed, our boat sucked all the water from under him, then when the water went back in it washed his boat out on the bank or sunk his boat.

5. Bosses & People with Money

Tugboat designed to tow barges behind / you can also push barges.

THE BOSSY WIFE

In Texas City, I boarded a boat. A woman was standing there on the dock. I knew who she was. She asked if I was going to be the Captain. I said, "That's what your husband told me."

She pulled out a sheet of paper that had a drawing of four barges and the boat. She said, "This is the way I want the boat-tow made up." On each barge she had E or L.

I said, "What does those stand for?"

"Empty and loaded."

I said, "In other words, you want the two loads out front."

"That's right."

My suitcase was still sitting on the deck. I reached down and picked it up and was leaving the dock when her husband drove up. He said, "Where are you going?"

"Trinity, Texas. Your wife just took my place."

He said, "Wait a minute." He went and told her to go home.

I got on the boat and everything was going fine when on our way back to Texas City, she called by marine operator. She said, "How have you got those barges made up?"

I called her by her name and told her to run her cook stove and I would run the boat. I then called her husband to be sure to have me a relief when we got to Texas City, because when the boat leaves Texas City I won't be on it. He already knew I was supposed to get off when we got back, but I didn't want him to forget. His bookkeeper had a full time job completing W-2 forms.

FREE LUNCH

When I got off the boat at Texas City there was a man waiting for me. He said, "My Captain had to have surgery and I need you for about two weeks, or longer if you want to stay."

I said, "When and where?"

"Here in about two days and I will call you," he said.

I said, "I'll make two trips which will be about fourteen days." I also gave him a date, which would be my last day regardless of where I was. This would be my last day to work. I was looking to get off after the second trip, but the date wasn't here yet. I left on the boat, but I told him when that date arrived I would be getting off wherever it was. I don't think he believed me.

We were southbound on the Plaquemine—Morgan City, Louisiana route when that date came. When we went through the railroad bridge at Morgan City, I told the mate to back up in the bridge, because I was getting off. I walked to the Morgan City side to the bus depot. I didn't have the money to buy a ticket home. I had enough to get me to Liberty, Texas with nickel left over. I called my wife and she was to meet me in Liberty.

I had about six hours before my bus came. There were six or seven men sitting around a big table outside the bus station chatting. I sat in a chair close by and they got me in their conversation. It was time to eat. They invited me to join them. I couldn't with a nickel in my pocket. I said, "I don't want to miss my bus." I also told one of them why I couldn't go.

"That's alright we will take care of it," they all agreed.

We loaded down in two cars. We went way back into the Bayou's to a big tin building. There weren't many cars. We went inside and sat in folding chairs and tables about ten feet long. They had any kind of seafood you wanted. A tray about two feet long and about eighteen inches wide on little wheels carried food. It slid up and down the table for people to help themselves. If one type of food was getting low, a waitress would refill the tray. When we finished eating and it was time to pay, they had a deck of cards and they cut them. I said, "Don't look at me." The low card paid for the meal.

We went back to the bus station. I thanked them all and they left. It was 1:00 PM and my bus was due in thirty minutes. The bus had a flat and was over an hour late. When the station master came to tell me about the flat, he also told me something else. He said, "You don't know it, but you had lunch with six of the richest men in Louisiana."

I said, "Who are they?"

When he started telling me the companies they owned, I knew what he was talking about. Before the bus got there, the men started coming back to sit around the table. I had a nickel so I bought a coke. I knew I wouldn't want anything to eat before I got to Liberty. The bus came and we left Morgan's City. When we got to our first rest stop I'd wished I hadn't spent my last nickel for a coke when I did.

I felt in my pocket to see if I might have missed one. I felt some paper and pulled it out and there were two twenty dollar bills. I got me a coke. We all got back on the bus. There was a lady sitting next to me. I'd tried to get a conversation all the way from Morgan's City. She never said a word. We past a big graveyard, I leaned over and pointed to the graveyard and said, "Did you know that people were just dying to go out there?"

We went down the road maybe ten miles when she said, "Where do think they would be?" I had messed up. She never shut her mouth from there to Liberty. I was glad to get off.

SALTY MONEY

We took two barges to Weeks Island to load with salt and had to wait on the barges. I was out on the dock walking around. This older man who wore a khaki suit came walking down the hill. When he got to me, we started talking about salt. We talked for some time when he left. After he was gone one of the men on the dock said, "Do you know who that was?"

I said, "No."

He said, "That's one of the owners. He owns more of company stock than any other stockholder."

I asked, "What's he doing down here?"

"He likes it down here. You should see his office wall; he has all kinds of degrees. You can bet your bottom dollar when there is a stock meeting he will be there."

NO MONEY

The Port Captain of a company in Houston called and wanted to know if I would go to St. Louis with a two-barge tow and I said that I would. He asked if I knew of a deckhand. I told him about my wife's uncle who had decked for me before. He and I went to Port Arthur, Texas, to get on the boat. We did pretty well until we hit the river. It was a slow boat to St. Louis. When the boat made it to St. Louis the owner decided to make a few trips up the Illinois River with the boat, so he sent a few of us a relief. He had sent them up on a train. I called and wanted to know where the rest of our train tickets were. He said I just furnish transportation to the boat; it's up to you to get home. *Was I mad?*

Between my wife's uncle and me we might have had ten dollars. We got off at St. Louis shipyard. We'd already decided we were going to hitchhike home. We left the shipyard walking. There was a train track with a train on it. A trainman was at the crossing. My wife's uncle asked him if the train was headed for Chicago. Unfortunately, was headed for the Rio Grande Valley. The trainman left and we threw our suitcases in a boxcar and got in. The train pulled out. After we rode for a while, we decided we were going in the right direction.

When we arrived in Arkansas, hunger set in. The train stopped to drop off some cars in some little town. There was a store not far off. My train partner ran and bought some cheese and crackers and a coke. We stayed on the train until it got to Palestine, Texas. We were only about sixty-five miles from our home so we got off because we didn't know where that car was going. About the time our feet hit the ground a railroad detective got us. He took us into the depot and a woman was there who worked in Trinity, Texas, where we lived.

She asked, "Henry, what are you doing here?" The detective gave her the details. She asked him if she gave us the money to ride a bus would he let us go. He agreed. We left the depot and I called my wife to come and get us.

The next day after we got home, I went to see the man that hired me. I was bluffing and I hoped it worked. "I'll be back in a little while," I said.

"Where are you going?"

"To the labor board."

"Hold on a minute," he said, then left. He was back in a few minutes. "What do you think we owe you?"

I said, "Three hundred dollars apiece."

He said, "Let me get the checks."

"I want cash. I don't want you to put a cancellation on a check."

He came up with six hundred dollars. He fixed out a paper for us to sign. I could only get three hundred dollars, because the other man wasn't there to sign for his three hundred dollars. I called my wife and told her to bring her uncle down there. I didn't leave until the other man got there a couple of hours later. We got three hundred dollars each and then we left.

A few months later, he had the gall to call me and wanted me to ride a train to Pittsburgh—to ride one of his boats south. I asked, "Did he know that there were airplanes that flew into Pittsburgh?" and I hung up.

HITCHHIKER

I was to get on the boat before Christmas at Memphis; I lived north of Houston and was going to fly. All flights into Memphis were cancelled because of snow and ice. I decided I would ride the bus. I got to Shreveport, Louisiana, and all bus runs were cancelled north and south because of ice and snow. I couldn't even get back home. I took a cab out to the road home. I was going to hitchhike if there were any cars moving. The cab driver let me out at a service station. I could see if any cars were coming. The first car stopped and picked me up. It was two brothers trying to get to Corpus Christi. Top speed was about forty miles an hour for about 125 miles. I got home about 3:00 PM.

PLANES

My youngest son got on the boat with me to ride for a while. The first place he'd go would be the galley. I had to go right on watch. He came to the pilot-house. He said, "Daddy, those refrigerators are just like the one we got at home."

I said, "They are."

He said, "Because they don't have anything in them." He rode the boat with me until it was time for me to get off.

We got off at Alton, Illinois. They picked us up early, because we had an early flight. When we got to the bridge across the Mississippi River, there was a wreck on the bridge. We were there three or four hours before we got through. We had missed our flight. We were put on a later flight. We boarded the plane and sat there for a while, but then they took us off. Something was wrong. We sat around until they had another plane. We taxied out, the engines revved up and we started down the runway. The pilot cut the engines trying to stop, and ran onto a field. All chutes and doors were open and they got us off the plane as soon as they could. There was a bomb threat.

We were waiting on buses to pick us up. Both these buses got within a hundred feet of the plane and then stopped. I told my son, "I don't believe this." This was after dark. I called my wife early in the day to make sure the car was filled with gas so she could come get us. She told my other son to fill the car up.

We got on another plane and didn't leave the gate; they pulled us off and put us on another plane. I'd had about all this I wanted for one day. After it was checked out, we were put on the plane that earlier had the bomb threat. We finally got out of St. Louis. When we got to Dallas, I called my wife to come get us. My other son forgot to fill up the car so my wife didn't have the gas to come and get us. She went across the road at 3:00 AM and borrowed some lawnmower gas to get her to an all-night station. She picked us up about twenty-four hours after we got off the boat. My son won't ride a plane today and this has been years and years ago.

Later, I had got off the boat at Louisville, Kentucky; I had reservations on a plane that I was to catch to Dallas. The one I had reservations on stopped in Nashville, Memphis, Little Rock to Dallas. I usually called my wife and gave her the flight and time I would be in Dallas. There was a flight that left two hours later that was a through flight that got to Dallas about the same time.

A man came to the ticket agent and wanted to go to Nashville. They had no vacancies so I told the agent if she could get me on the through flight to Dallas she could give this man my seat to Nashville. She got me on the other flight. Since they were arriving in Dallas at the same time I didn't see any need to call my wife. I made it to Dallas and looked for my wife—I couldn't find her. I called home and my son answered the phone. The first thing he said, "So, you've gone to Cuba for a vacation."

I didn't catch what he said. "Where is mother?" I asked.

"She is on her way back home. Why?"

"When mother got to Dallas she found out the flight you was supposed be on was hijacked to Cuba, so, she turned around and is on her way home."

"Okay. When she gets there tell her I will rent a car to come home."

6. Bad Crews and Tiny Shirts

ANOTHER CLOSE CALL

We ran twenty-four hours a day as long as weather and channel permitted us to go. There were boat stores along the river. They had a barge with fuel that would fuel our boat, so we never had to stop. The boat stores had a boat to bring groceries out and they would make our crew changes for us. When I started, there were three boat stores—Wood River, Illinois; Memphis, Tennessee; and Baton Rouge, Louisiana. In Baton Rouge, you had to tie your boat-tow off and go get fuel.

There were also grocery stores. You called your order in and they'd bring our groceries down to the bank. They would put them on your boat-tow, or you could send your "run-about" boat to the shore to get them. Now there are more places to get groceries and fuel.

I was pumping a barge of gasoline in Corpus Harbor when a ship was turning around and hit the barge, breaking it loose from dock and breaking the pumping hose. I saw what was happening and broke in a run to shut the pump engine down. The hose broke just before I got to the engine to shut it down. What kept it from catching a fire, I will never know. Both the engine and I were sprayed with gasoline and the engine was hot. It was the next day before I got my color back. I don't know if I've ever been so scared.

***

Back in the early fifties, there weren't many boats with power steering in the Intracoastal, it was all wheel work. One boat had an air motor hooked up to a Model A transmission. The transmission was connected to a shaft that went to the rudder. The transmission and motor was under the pilothouse floor. We could pull up part of the floor and change gears. If we were boat-towing empty barges we put it in second, or third. If we were pushing loads, we would put it in first. There was an engineer that wanted to be a pilot. I would let him steer. I would put the transmission in reverse, and when he turned the lever to go one way, it would go the other. It would only be a minute and he'd be all over the canal. I told him it took a lot more upstairs to steer a boat than work in the engine room. One day I left it in first gear because we had loads. I called him by name and told him I had all the faith in him this time. He went on to make a pilot.

***

We were tied off at Lemont, Illinois. From there on the bridges were too low to go under. You turned your boat tow over to a retractable pilot-house boat. At the time, we were the only ones tied up there. There were three or four of us sitting on the lower deck and there was a boat coming up behind us. He had plenty of room to pass. Boats had been passing us for two days while we were waiting on our barges. For some reason he hit us on the stern of our boat, the ropes we were tied off broke and hitting all us that was sitting there. Two went to the hospital and when I came to I was still lying on the deck. They had put some blankets under me, but I didn't have any broken bones. They took me on to the hospital, but released me after I could walk a straight line.

I and others were sitting in the galley. One deckhand said, "Henry, you have been telling what can happen if a line breaks and hits you. We believed you and really don't think you needed to demonstrate this to us."

I felt like hitting him in mouth, even I knew he was

kidding. The two in the hospital were beat up and bruised one had a broken arm the other had a broken leg and a few other things. They both returned to work later on.

DIRTY ROTTEN THIEVES

We had one barge of pressurized anhydrous ammonia going to Harlingen, Texas. It was hot and the heat caused the pop off valves to let the pressure off. We had gas masks with us all time. We had to put the mask on when it popped off. We had a little two-inch pump. We got it and started spraying the tanks down with water to help them cool them off. It stopped them from popping off. It didn't take long for me to get as much of this as I could stand. There are better things to do than wear a gas mask in south Texas in July or August.

This was the first load of anhydrous ammonia to go into Harlingen. My brother had taken the first load of gasoline to Harlingen when they opened the canal to Brownsville, Texas. They threw a party when the first load of new product came into Harlingen. When I went in there, they had a vegetable auction during the day and a dance all night. There were thousands of acres of vegetables auctioned at a time. We stayed there several days.

I was working for two brothers. When they brought the supplies to the boat both would come.

The captain said, "I don't know where all the supplies are going. This happens every time they bring supplies." The Captain would check them off as they were put on board. When the supplies were loaded, one brother would get everybody on the other side of the boat. The other brother would load about half the supplies back in their truck. I told the captain what was happening to the supplies, but he wouldn't believe me. He had been with them since they started in business. So he would just let it go, and take the chewing for using too many supplies. After I left, he caught them and he quit.

STEALING AND SECOND CHANCES

We had a cook who acted suspiciously when she got off the boat. She lived between Memphis and Greenville, and would get off at Memphis with her suitcase and have a box put off at Greenville. I looked into it.

About six hours before we got to Memphis, I went and looked in the deep freezes and made note of what was there. Later, when everybody was on deck to get off, I looked in the deep freezes and checked again. I hurried on deck and picked up her suitcase, as if to help. It was too heavy just for clothes and I popped it open. It was full of frozen meat! She didn't say a word, just got on the store boat, leaving her suitcase behind. I don't know where she went.

The cook is not the only one who would steal groceries. The cook came to me and said that she had package of T-bone steaks missing.

I said, "When was the last time she saw them?"

"About an hour ago."

We had one person getting off. I walked outside before the store boat came along side. I asked a deckhand would he happen to have a package of fourteen T-bone steaks in his suitcase. From the look on his face I knew he had them. I said, "You got about five minutes before the boat gets here. You can go to the deck locker, put them over behind those barrels and after you get off, I will put them back in the deep freeze."

That's what he did. When he started to get on the store boat he asked, "Am I fired?"

I said, "Have you learned anything?"

"I sure have," he answered.

"This is between you and I. Nobody will ever know about this from me and we will see you in thirty days."

Under normal conditions, I would have fired the boy then and there. But he was a good boy, hard worker and all you had to do is tell him one time. He didn't forget. When it was time for him to come on watch, he was always ready waiting on the mate.

I knew his conditions at home. A man from the same town told me. His daddy ran off with another woman, leaving behind four children, three younger than this deckhand. His mother was sick and the burden was on him for the family needs. When he got off the boat, he worked for a man in his hometown eight to twelve hours a day to put food on the table and clothes on his family back.

I took the T- bone steaks and put them under some other meat. The next day the cook told me she had put some other meat on top of the steaks.

I was off the boat when he came back, but I got on in a few days. As soon as I got on the boat, he said he would like to talk to me.

I said, "When I get off watch come to my room." When he came to my room, he was almost crying.

He said, "I have never stole anything in my life. I am ashamed of what I did and started not to come back and face you. This chance you gave me, you will never regret it."

He told me he wanted to be a pilot. One day I let him steer the boat and he did a good job. I let him steer a lot after that until I quit or went to another boat. A few years later he was bringing a barge line tow with loaded barges south on the Mississippi.

He told me he would never get married until his brother and sisters were out of school and college if they wanted to go. He stuck with his word. He had a sixth grade education and he wanted his sisters and brother to have an education. About six months after his youngest sister got her college degree he got married. About six months after he got married, he was killed in a car wreck.

Sometimes giving a person a second chance doesn't hurt. I have given a few the second chances that I was glad that I did. I had always believed in giving a person a second chance. I have had some second chances myself.

JAILBIRD WINOS

The company I worked for called and wanted to know if I would make a trip to Lake Charles for a company that did some boat towing for them some times. I said that I would. I went to Galveston to get on the boat. There was a man on the boat when the owner showed up. He asked, "Are you ready to go?"

"Where's the rest of the crew?"

He said, "I only keep an engineer on the boat and I'll go get the rest of the crew."

He came back. He went to the jail to get the rest of the crew. They were all experienced people, but wine-o jailbirds.

The engineer started the engine; we went to pick up a barge to go to Lake Charles. I was going down the canal, when a boat behind me called and said one of your crew just got off. I looked back; the crewmember was just getting out on the bank with his bag. When I got to West Port Arthur, Texas Bridge, there were three of us left.

I called the owner, to tell him.

"Can you make it on to Lake Charles and I will have some more crew," he asked.

When we got to Lake Charles, he found crew members from another company. The barge was loaded and we took it back to Houston. I took the boat up to the company dock and tied it off. I told my boss to never call me to make another trip on that boat. The owner did give me an extra hundred dollars, which was about three days' pay—back then. I never made another trip on that boat.

Years later I found out the boat had belong to his father and he had died, the son wasn't interested in boats when I made the trip for him. The son sold his own business—whatever it was—and went in the boat business fulltime, working off shore drilling rigs. He got the right contracts and built a fleet of offshore supply boats—so I was told.

VINDICATED

I was working on a retractable pilot-house boat. About our fourth trip, we went into Chicago and the Captain, who thought he was the Captain of the Battleship Missouri, decided to turn the boat around a different way. He knew the way he was turning he was putting the stern of the boat in a bad place. There was a sign where an old dock had been and there were a lot of pilings below water. He hit one, knocked a rudder off and bent the propeller.

We were coming out of Chicago with eleven hundred feet of empty barges, one rudder one propeller bent so badly you couldn't speed the engine up. We were still in the Chicago canal when Lockport locks called and I was told to call the office.

When we got to the lock I did just that. They started chewing me out for knocking the rudder off and bending the propeller. I said, "Just hold on. I didn't do that."

"The Captain told me you did."

"You talk to the crew on the boat because I will be getting off in Joliet Harbor." I knew I had to get off because the Captain and I would have it out for him lying about me. I went back to the boat and told him to let me off at the last bridge in Joliet, Harbor.

There was snow everywhere and I got off with about twenty dollars in my pocket—this was before credit cards. I walked to the train depot and decided I would buy a ticket as far as the twenty dollars would go. It would get me down in Arkansas somewhere. I was still debating where to get my wife to wire me some money. It would be the next day before I got it.

An older woman sat down beside me—she was in her seventies. She said, "You look worried about something."

"I'm not worried. Just trying to figure out how to get home."

She asked, "You live in Texas, don't you? And there is a lot of cross-ties between here and there. My husband worked for the railroad and he was always saying there is a lot of cross-ties between here and there."

"How do you know I am from Texas?" I asked.

"The way you talk," she said. She asked where I was headed and if I had any money.

"Twenty-dollars," I told her.

She went to the ticket window. She came back with me a ticket. I was going to give her the twenty dollars.

She said, "You have a long layover in St. Louis and you will need to eat."

"Give me your address and I'll send you the money," I requested.

"You don't owe me anything, because it didn't cost me anything."

She asked if I would watch her bag. I said that I would and I got her address and phone number off her bag.

I waited until the next year before Mother's Day. I mailed her the nicest mother day card I could find and a twenty-dollar bill and told her to buy her some chocolates. She wrote me a letter thanking me for the card and sent my twenty-dollars back saying chocolates were fattening.

When I got home the office had called me. I was tired so I waited until I rested up before I would call them back. They called me again.

The boss said, "I have talked to everyone one on the boat and they said you were in the galley when the Captain backed into those pilings."

They paid my way home plus the two days to get home. They put me on another boat. The consultant called and said his time was up he'd be leaving.

TIDE™ & THE COASTGUARD

The first winter I ran into Chicago, we were hauling heavy oils and asphalt. While we were pumping off, a hose busted and a lot of oil went into the Chicago canal. They called the Coast Guard. When the Coast Guard arrived they saw what a mess we had. The Coast Guard in charge told the

Captain to get all the Tide washing powder he could. When the washing powder arrived, the Coast Guard told the Captain to sprinkle the washing powder on the oil. In an hour, there was no trace of oil. That washing powder made the heavy oil sink. We had washing powder left over, but we kept it on board.

Years later, I was in Texas City where they had a spill. They were lucky because the wind was out of the south and it kept the oil in a slip. One night, I was passing by in my car when I saw them looking and I could tell what was up. I asked the Captain if he have any Tide. He said that he had some.

"Throw some on the oil and see what happens," I said.

They put the washing powder on the oil; the oil started sinking right away. We went to the boat store and put all the tide we could in my car. The dock had called the game warden and the Coast Guard. By the time the game warden got there, there was no trace of oil. They couldn't find any oil, so nothing happened. When I was Captain and we were hauling heavy oil, I always had plenty of Tide on the boat.

WEATHER

If you have a high tide when a norther blows in and you are in open water it can break all the cables and rope you have holding the boat to the barges and the barges together. We knew a norther was about to blow in and we were waiting for it to blow in before we crossed Galveston Bay. You could see it coming. I was on a 3200-horsepower boat, with three or four barges. Another riverboat passed us. I called the other Captain and ask did he know a norther was about to hit. He told me they didn't worry about something like that, because they had plenty of rigging to hold the barges together.

As he started to make the turnout of the canal in Galveston Bay to head up the Houston Ship Channel, the norther blew in. He had out too much rigging. Whatever rigging that didn't break, pulled the deck fitting it was fastened to, off the barges, and bent one of his boat tow knees on the boat. That is what you put up against the barges to push your barges with. The barges had to go to the shipyard to get the deck fitting replaced before they could be loaded. He lost all his barges, one hit a ship and one went to the gulf. I don't remember where the others went. When there are twelve or more boat tows waiting on the weather you just don't pass them. If you get out there and get in trouble you are on your own. Don't call one of those waiting boats to help you. You are wasting your breath.

Instead of waiting eighteen hours or less, he lost about a week. The barges had to be gas freed, more fittings put on the barges, and a new boat tow knee made and put on.

I met him on the river when he was telling me what happened. He said that he called the dispatcher and told him they were going to need to wait on the weather before crossing Galveston Bay. The dispatcher told him to double up all his rigging and go. He did, and then the company saw what the results were, when they got their bills for the damage, plus the loss time. I asked, "Does the dispatcher still had a job?"

I was told he was still in the office.

If that had been me, I would have told the dispatcher or the owner, "No." *Why?* I had the experience and I knew what could happen. I'd been on the deck and pilot-house when a norther blew in. When I went out on the river I listened to people who had the experience. When I retired I was still doing the same thing. I like to talk, but if I heard boat people talking to one another about certain places I was all ears.

***

We were coming down the Atchafalaya River and there was a hurricane coming in between New Orleans and Morgan's City. We stopped about forty miles above Morgan's City. We had four barges—two wide and two long. We missed the hurricane, but not the tornados. One came through and everything that wasn't bolted or welded down on off two barges. The other two barges—there wasn't a thing moved

***

When we first started getting good radars, we ran a lot in the fog. This is when you make a judgment call. If I was coming down the river and it got foggy, if I had room to turn around I would turn around and back through the bridge. I did this when I had an empty unit boat tow. When running in fog during daytime you keep your head in a hood where you can see the radar. If you pull your head out of the hood and then put your head back into the hood, it takes a few minutes for your eyes to adjust.

I was northbound with about 1100 feet of boat tow. It was about 9:00 AM and it was still shut-out fog. I was trying to get lined up for a bridge on the Illinois River. I pulled my head out of to see if the fog had cleared and what time it was. Still shut-out fog, so I went back trying to line up to get through the bridge.

A few minutes later the engineer walked in and wanted to know what I was doing. "Trying to line this bridge up."

"Henry, if you will get out of the way I'll make this bridge for you. I looked up and it didn't look like there had ever been any fog.

***

We came down above the Baton Rouge Bridge running in shut-out fog. I'd already come around Wilkerson Point when I heard a horn blow one time and I answered. I tried to get him on the radio, the horn blew again and I answered. My radar wasn't picking up anything below the bridge—which wasn't unusual because of the bridge.

The cook walked up and asked, "Henry, what are you doing?"

I said, "There's a boat below the bridge and I can't get him on the radio."

She said, "That's no boat. It's a foghorn on the bridge."

I sat there and listened. Every so often it would blow. I eased on through the bridge feeling quite stupid.

***

When I began running the Ohio River, I didn't know how fast it would rise or fall. This was when the radar didn't work half the time and it more or less just gave you the shore line. The fog set in and it was thick. The captain got up to see what was going on. I could get a line to tie the boat tow off. We were right beside a river light. He said drop back down the river about a thousand feet because the river is falling and there is a sand bar here. I backed down the river about a thousand feet. He and a deckhand went out to check out how much water we had stopped in. He came back and said we have about fourteen feet of water all the way round the barges. The river was not going to fall fast enough.

It was almost noon before the fog lifted. We took the line off the tree. We were aground. He said the river had fell four feet while we were tied off. There must have been a hump under the barge.

We finally got off ground. From that day on I would move my boat tow about every hour on a falling river. You learn from your mistakes.

***

In 1957, Hurricane Audrey started out in the Gulf of Mexico, It caught everybody off guard. It moved on shore so fast the people in Cameron, Louisiana, didn't have a chance to make it to the mainland. There was a pontoon bridge across the Gulf Intracoastal Waterways. The tide got so high the bridge couldn't be used by cars. People were driving their cars to the bridge and walking across, until the tide got so high they couldn't do that. We were the last boat tow to lock through Calcasieu Locks. We managed to get to the Sabine River close to Orange, Texas, where we would have a little protection. We tied off in a bunch of trees. We had a number of lines to the shore to tie the barges and boat off. We took rope or wire and tied all the doors shut so they wouldn't blow open. Everybody went to the forward part of the engine room away from any glass. It seemed like the boat would come up out of the water then drop. When the wind died down where I could go look out, our boat had broken loose from the barges, and the barges were gone; we were just floating around. We had floated about a half mile from where we were tied off. All the cables that were holding the barges together had broken. There was an opening where three of the barges had blown up against some trees. When we found the fourth and about half of it was on the bank. We got the three barges then went where the fourth was. The deckhands put a number of ropes between the three barges and the fourth barge. They left a lot of slack so we could jerk the barge along. After about fifteen or twenty jerks, it was in the water.

The wind was still blowing pretty hard. We still couldn't go anywhere with the wind blowing and us with empty barges. We lost a few windows and tree limbs were all over the boat and barge. There was no other real damage except a bunch of broke cables and ropes and a tree had fell on one of the main cargo pump engines. The cook said that half of her dishes were broken. Still, we had a very little damage compared to a lot of others.

I called the company and told them everything. I asked if I could I hire a harbor boat to help us from where we were through the west Port Arthur Bridge. I wasn't worried then about the hurricane, it was the tornados, and I wanted to get as far west as I could. They hired a boat to help us. The tide had dropped where water was in the banks on the west side of the west Port Arthur Bridge. There had been very little sleep in the last two days or so. The pilot was on watch when we got through the bridge. I had gone to sleep, but the engines woke me up. I couldn't figure out what the pilot was doing so I got up to see. The wind was still blowing too hard to push the barges. The pilot had taken the boat around on the other end of the boat tow and backing up with the boat tow. We backed from Port Arthur to Bolivar, Texas which was about fifty miles.

***

In 1961, an oil company had some barges either leaving Houston going to Corpus Christi or the other way round. I was working for the company that was towing these three barges with another boat. I was called to go get on the boat. I refused because there was a strong hurricane working out it the Gulf. I told the owner I would not go because of the hurricane. They had it pinpointed between Brownsville and Galveston. The owner got mad and I quit. I was told those three loaded barges went out in the flats west of Port O'Connor.

JUST BEING HENRY

This pilot was working with me. Every time he came on the boat he would have new shirts by the time he got off they would be tight. He didn't gain weight. There was an engineer that was smaller than the pilot. When the pilot started to get off the engineer would buy the shirts for twenty five, or fifty cents each.

We had a commercial washer and dryer which would get extra hot; they were in a room that joined the engine room. Our icemaker broke and we got a new one. The engineer took the old one to the engine room and got it working a little. I got curious and the pilot washed his clothes before coming on watch. I had an idea what was happening, but not sure. I went down to eat and then went to the washing room and hid. A few minutes later here comes the engineer with a five-gallon bucket of ice and a little water. The engineer stopped the dryer, turned it up as high as it would go and let run a little a while. He took those shirts put them in the ice water. He took the shirts out of the ice water and put them in the dryer. He did this twice. When the pilot went to put one of the shirts on it was tight. He said that he couldn't figure out what happened. The next time he washed, he found out somebody had turned the dryer up on high when he went to get his clothes out of the dryer. He figured out who it was.

***

One of the engineers and pilot were good friends. If you put a lock on something, they had to know what you had in there. I got an old apple box. It had a bottom, top and door. I put four or five bricks inside and put a lock on it and then shoved it up against the wall. It didn't have a back on the box. They kept after me to tell them what I had in the box. I refused them time and again. Then, each one offered me five dollars to show them what I had in there. I refused. It got up to ten dollars each. I refused. When I had the twenty dollars in my hand, I gave in. We went down to my room and I pulled box away from the wall so they could see in the back. All they saw was the brick. Before they got off I gave them their money back.

***

I was working for this company that had four or five boats. There was a deckhand that worked for me on all of them. He came to me down in the dumps, looking sad. I said, "What is the matter with you?"

"Did they tell you my grandma passed away? I would like to get off."

I said, "Sure."

He got off and went home. A few months later we were on a different boat. A deckhand woke me up and told me that this same fellow's grandma died and he had to get off.

I asked him, "Just how many grandmas did you have?" His answer was each time was, "I want to get off the boat."

I said, "Don't forget your last grandma has died with me."

***

I hired a deckhand in Memphis; the first thing he asked me was what would happen if he died on the boat. There was no problem there.

"I keep extra-large new flags in my room. We take his body and lay it out on deck, roll him good in the flag then you see that big thing over there, that is an extra-large ratchet we tie that to him then throw him over the side and let the catfish take care of him."

He went down stairs and talked to the cook. She told him, "They would get you off the boat to the nearest boat town then next of kin would take it from there."

He came back to the pilot-house to tell me what a lie I had told him. He told me he had talked to the cook and she told me what would take place. He got married and he told his wife what happen if he died on the boat. He told her what I told him. She told him to find him another job. He tried to tell her he was just kidding. He had to quit.

***

I was on a retractable pilot-house boat on a big hydraulic ram. When you get to a bridge the pilot-house won't go under, you hit a button, or leaver and the pilot-house drops.

I was on watch and I noticed now and then, the pilot-house would shake like we were hitting bottom. I looked out the back door to the stairs that would go down when the pilot-house did. There were two men standing there talking. Now, and then they would grab hold of the ladder and stretch. When they did the pilot-house would move. I didn't mention this to anyone.

We were going up river with a loaded tow. I got by the ladder and shook it; the captain grabbed the throttles and slow down. I stepped under the pilot-house where he couldn't see me. He sped up. I went on about my never mind for about a week. We were coming down above a bridge when I shook the pilot-house, I could hear him cursing above the noise of the engine. After this I wasn't about to tell him what I'd done.

7. Tankerman License

Making Vicksburg, Mississippi Bridge with 25 loaded barges

After I had got my tankerman license, I was steaming a barge in Houston on December the 23rd. I'd never steamed a barge before. The company had about six shore tanker men. I asked two of them the best way to steam a barge. All they told me was to open all the steam valves and let it go. When pure steam started coming out, cut down on the discharge valve.

The dock man was an older man who thought I was taking too long. He said, "Son, the way you're steaming this barge, you won't be home until next Christmas!" Then he helped me.

We shut everything off except the number one tanks. When we got pure steam on the number one tanks, we cut down on the discharge to build up pressure. There was a lot of water at first, but when we got pure steam, we opened up number two. Four hours after we had pure steam on the number one tanks, we started pumping. I got home Christmas Eve.

This old man taught me a great deal and I did a lot of barge steaming. I used this for years on heavy oils. When the company saw how much faster I could steam a barge, I got a lot more work. I did a lot of barge steaming for the refinery where this older fellow worked. Over the years, I learned something else: very few people knew how to steam a barge.

***

The company sent me to Port Arthur, Texas, to steam some heavy oil. I set the steam up and had it going. The captain on the boat saw what I was doing. He told me to open up the other tanks. I picked my coat up and was about to leave.

He said, "Where are you going?

"Home."

He ask, "Why?"

I said, "The Company sent me over here to steam the barges and since you want to steam them, have at it."

He said, "No, I want to know what about the other tanks."

I said, "Why don't you watch me?" and he did.

That was a regular run for this boat. It took three days to steam and pump. I didn't do the pumping, just the steaming. I already had steam on number two tanks. After about five hours, I told the tankerman he could start pumping. He said that there was no way the oil was hot enough to pump. He went to look at the gauges, and then started pumping. Before he had half, number one tanks were pumped out and number two's were ready to pump. In twenty-nine hours, the two barges were pumped off. I stayed up the whole time. The captain stayed up and just watched me. He made a remark to me about how they had been steaming. I had told him that he couldn't just turn the steam on and forget about it. You had to stay on top of it. If he saw a little water coming out, open the steam discharge valve to blow the water out. Steaming a barge is like a dog that won't bite; you have to keep your eye on it all time and make sure you have live steam coming out of the discharge, but hold as much pressure on the steam coils as possible and still have steam coming out of the discharge.

The captain and I got to talking about a man I'd known for years—I'd decked for him. He told me that over the time he had been hauling heavy oil and the tankermen he had, he had never seen a barge steamed like that.

"Just stop and think a minute; you are not going to pump all your tanks at one time so, why steam all the tanks at one time?"

He said that made sense and he learned something from a man half his age. You are never too old to learn.

NEPOTISM

I was docking a barge at Norco, Louisiana. The port captain was on the boat. He was one of those people who knew everything, but really knew nothing. He did not know I had shifted barges in and out of that dock a number of times. He was related to the owner's wife. He came to the pilothouse and said, "Henry, it takes special knowledge to put a barge behind this dock. You had better let me do it."

There was a deckhand that witnessed this and I motioned him to leave. When we got downstairs, I told the deckhand the way the port captain was going at it he was going to demolish the inside of the dock. Not only did he tear the dock up, he knocked a big hole in the barge and let the stern of the boat hit the bank, knocking off both rudders. I had no idea this man had never operated a boat, because I was just tripping on the boat.

I couldn't keep my mouth shut. After it was all said and done, I told him I have been putting barges behind this dock for years, and I am glad I don't have your knowledge to do it, and then I left. This was done on my watch and the owner thought I did it. The port captain lied about the accident. When we got to Avondale Shipyard, the owner was there. I got the port captain, deckhand and the owner together. We got it straight the first thing, the owner told his relative to stay away from the controls. That's when I found out the port captain had been only a delivery man and had no experience in handling a boat. I've always been one to get something straight while it was fresh on everybody's mind.

8. Any Great Ideas?

PROBLEM SOLVER

We had a barge come off dry dock and we were loading gasoline. The tankerman came to me because the Captain was in bed. He said, "I got gasoline coming in a tank. I don't have the valve open on."

I went out and put my head down in the loading hatch and knew it wasn't gasoline. I told him to tell the dock man to stop loading. I woke the Captain up and told him what happened.

He said, "Call the office and leave me alone."

I called the office and two men came down, and then a man from the shipyard. I'd learned something in the service that was of some use here. I needed a bolt, two steel washers, two lead washers, and a nut for the bolt. They were talking about pumping the gas off and putting the barge back on dry dock. This meant pumping the gas off that we'd loaded, a couple days gas freeing, repairing the hole, and loading the gasoline.

They realized that when they cut a hole in the bottom of the tank to drain the water out, they forgot to weld it up. We were looking at a three-day delay. I called the big boss to one side and said, "I'm proposing an idea. I don't know if it'll work, but it's worth a try."

After he heard my suggestion he said, "Let's go for it. What will you need?"

"A broom handle, two three-to-four inch lead washers, two steel washers, about an inch larger than the lead, one inch bolts, nuts, and fifty feet of quarter-inch rope."

While the man went after the stuff, the water was pumped out. We started our cargo pump and pumped the water into a tank on the hill. There wasn't supposed to be any gas in the tank, but I put on a gas mask anyway.

I explained to the people what I was to do and what they were to do. I took the broom handle and rope with me. I cut a notch in the broom handle so that the rope would stay on. I put the rope through the hole and tied it to the broom handle. I used the wheel (propeller) to wash the broom handle out on the other side. When the rope came out, I took the rope, put a steel washer on the bolt first, then the lead washer, then wired the rope to the bolt and I pulled it under the barge through the hole. I put a lead washer on, then a steel washer, then the nut. They had sent me a 24" wrench to fit the nut and a pipe wrench to hold the bolt if it turned. There wasn't anything going through that hole when I tightened it up. Altogether, it took about three hours, and then we loaded our barge. We were told that the gasoline would eat through the lead washer. I had left the company, but I was told the bolt stayed in barge until the next dry dock inspection five years later.

When I finished the job, my boss opened his billfold and handed me a good size bill. The shipyard owner said, "You old tight wad." He then handed me several bills—a lot more than the boss gave me. My boss said he was going to get a relief for me and wanted to see me in the office as soon as I got off. I had no idea what this was about.

I went to the office and he said, "I want to go show you something. Go down and get on a certain boat and meet me at the Lynchburg ferry by the San Jacinto Monument on the Houston Ship Channel."

I did as I was told and picked him up at the ferry landing and went up the San Jacinto River about a mile. There was an old wooden sea-going tug that the company owned that had been sunk for years. The Corp of Engineers had told them to get it out. The decks were out of the Water, but the boat was full of water.

He asked, “Can you float that thing? I’ve already got a salvage price. All the machinery is out of it.”

I said, “Let me get a boat and a certain barge and four or five 4” pumps, and four men. If those pumps won’t gain on it, get your salvage company. If we get it to float what are you going to do with it?”

“Let’s see if we can get it to float then I will cross that bridge.” I knew we had everything in our yard I would need.

We went to the dock office and got everything loaded. My boss was there watching and I told him I would like to be at the old tug at daylight. We sat a three hundred gallon tank on the barge and filled it with gas to run the pumps. He had people in the yard to check and make sure all the pumps were working. At 4:00 AM, five men showed up to go with me. We got our barge and took off. I was only about twenty-two or twenty-three at the time—stupid enough to try anything.

I called my older brother and asked him would he come down there to tell me how stupid I was. He lived over a hundred miles away. He got there shortly after we did. I explained what my intentions were.

He looked around then he said, “Take me back to the ferry landing and let me know how you come out. You know everybody in the company said it couldn’t be done—including me.”

I took him to the ferry landing and went back to the old tug. He put a little doubt in my mind, so I tried to forget about what he said.

They had all the pumps running including the barge pump which was eight inches. By noon it was pumped out to where we could see where the machinery set. At 4:00 PM we had all the water pumped out, but the boat hadn’t come up an inch. It had suction on the bottom. *How was I going to break this suction?* I called the boss and told him all of this. I told him it was dark and I was going to leave well enough alone until daylight. I asked could he have somebody pick up some of the men because we only had three bunks.

There was a little water coming in, but one pump would

keep it pumped out. We had just lain down when I thought of something. What if that thing broke suction and half the bottom of the boat fell off? About 3:00 AM, it broke suction and caused three people to come wide awake. The old boat had two cables to the shore. We all grabbed our flashlight and a little more water was coming in. We started four pumps and we were gaining on it. I called the boss and told him the tug was floating. He said to just keep it floating until I heard back from him. I asked for more people to help us. I also told him we needed to put a barge on both sides, before it was moved; he sent a little barge down there. I forgot to tell him we were going to need some cable to run under the boat to connect to the barge to hold it up if the bottom fell out.

There was a dry dock a few miles away that wasn't being used. He got it boat-towed to where the old tug was. Three days and a few hours after we first looked at the old tug it was on a dry dock. They got the dry dock boat-towed to the shipyard. It was dark when we got back to the dock office. The boss had another boat to pick up the equipment we used and I went to bed.

When the boss got in the office I went to see him. I joked, "I would like for you to figure out every penny it cost to get the boat in the dry dock, to see if I should go in the salvage business."

He gave me almost half a year's salary. I called my brother and told him the old tug was on dry dock. Just a few months later I quit, then my brothers quit. My boss told the personal man it would be a cold day in hell when another Elliott worked for him. We didn't do anything, but quit with a two weeks' notice. He was on vacation when I quit. He did call me a few months later and wanted to know why we quit. I didn't tell him, but they had put a man in charge for some of the operation that I and a lot of other people didn't agree with.

About two weeks before I started on the old tug I sat on the bank and watched a salvage rig raise an old tug not over six hundred feet from my company property. That's where I came up with two barges and cables. When I'd seen the tug raised they put a barge on each side and run some cables under the old tug to the barges. I walked down there and ask why the cables? He told me. You connected two big cables to one barge then take a rope and run under the boat and pull the cables under the old tug. You then connected the other end of the cable to a barge one the other side of the tug. You did this after the tug was raised. The cables would keep the old tug from sinking if a bigger hole came in the tug before we got it on dry dock. That's what we did.

***

I was making a trip on a company boat and the Captain wouldn't get up. He would get up put his clothes on and go back to bed. It was always six-thirty before he got up there to relieve me. We were eastbound almost to Port O'Connor. They had dredged a slip where I could ease in and let the engine run slow to keep the barges in the slip. I had told a deckhand to wake the Captain up one time. I told the engineer to watch it for me. I went to bed. About 10 AM, the Captain woke up and saw I was in bed. He went to the pilot-house, backed out, and got underway. He was mad, but I didn't care.

The office called through the marine operator and wanted to know where we were. He told the office he wasn't awake. When we got our barges docked and we went to our dock office. I had already packed my clothes. I walked up to the dock office and there was the boss man. He got on me hard and heavy for not waking the Captain up. I said, "Wait until the Captain gets here then I will tell what happen and see if he has a different story than mine."

The Captain showed up. I said, "Let's get this out in the open." I told my story. He said nobody called him. I said, "Did you sleep in your clothes?"

The boss asked some of the other people that rode regular with him. Neither one of us got fired, but from that day on, all you had to do was open his door and he was up. I was told this because I never rode the boat with him again until years later when he was pilot on the boat where I was Captain. He was always up before time when he worked with me.

***

I thought there has to be a faster way to load. The company was getting about two loads a month out of there. The company had a barge with a piping arrangement; you could use the barge pump to load the barge itself. When I got back to Houston I went to see the boss man. I explained to him if they sent a certain barge down there they could suck the shore tanks dry in four or five hours. He said that is a big barge for 4000 barrels of oil. They sent this barge down there and I went down to load. Two hours and thirty minutes after we got the hoses connected and started loading, we had sucked their tanks dry. The company had been hauling oil out of this place for years. Why hadn't somebody figured this out before now? My idea was they could just lie around while the barge loaded, but why hadn't someone in the office figured it out?

While we were talking about barges, I said it wouldn't take that much work, to change the loading and discharge barge piping that they were using down there. (I forgot they would need to change to a different pump also). It was the size they needed to haul the oil instead of the one they had sent down there, because it was over twice the size as the one they had been using. It went alone for couple months; they sent the barge to the shipyard to change the piping arrangement they were also to change to a different type of pump. They spent the money on the barge piping and pump so they could use the barge to load with the barge pump. They took the barge back to the Corpus company dock. They took it to the dock to load. They couldn't get it to load by using the pump. I was off the boat, when they called and wanted me to go see why they couldn't use the pump to load. I drove six hundred miles round trip to open a valve. I didn't know when I had so much pleasure out of something.

This Captain was a regular know it all. I went up to the office and called our office and told them the barge pump was loading the barge. They asked me what I did and I told him. I understood they used the barge on other jobs also in the Corpus Christi area for different companies. If a company had a barge pump to break down the company would use the barge to pump other people's barges off for them.

AUTHORITIES

We were loading crude oil in the in barge where they didn't have a pump to load the oil on to the barge. It gravitated and it took about twenty-four hours to load four to five thousand barrels of oil. I noticed this man just walking around. After eight hours they would change watches. The barge was in a little slip that had been dredged to put barges to load.

These men just walked around the slip the eight hours. It finally got to me. I walked up to one of the men and asked what he was doing if it was any of my business. "We're game wardens."

This was my second trip and last time to go in there on a boat.

AGROUND

When I went to work on the river, a pilot or captain was just waiting to hit ground, because the channel changed so much and so fast. We had an empty tow of oil barges. I was behind a barge line boat tow. I was about an hour behind him. I was in the channel when my boat came to a sudden stop. My barge went on down the river. I backed up and went from one side of the channel and couldn't find water deep enough to get through. A boat down river caught my barges and tied them off. We sounded how wide the bar was. We found one place where we could wash out about ten feet and we would be in good water. I turned the boat around and eased back until the rudders hit the bar. I made sure my rudders were straight. I knew no harder than I hit the bar that it wouldn't damage the rudders or propellers. I started backing slow, sucking the sand out from behind us. It taken about forty-five minutes and we were in the clear. As soon as the boat cleared I stopped and turned the boat around, went on to get our barges, and continued south. They had to wait on a dredge to dredge the bar out. There were a number of boat tows north and southbound waiting before they got the channel open. There have been times when two boats would face up bow to bow and wash us out a channel.

This took place between Helena, Arkansas and Arkansas City. The channel was marked across the point way. We were following a northbound tow when he ran aground in the channel. We had started on the crossing and the river was falling. We had to back out and got along the shore. This boat that was aground couldn't get his barge off. The Captain tied our boat tow off and was going to help to try and get the barge off ground. There were three or four boats trying to free the barge. He broke his coupling between the grounded barge and backed out and tied the rest of his tow on the shore. We could not get the barge off ground. One or two other boats that was helping when we started out, we had trouble getting out.

Within six hours after he ran aground, there was about five feet of water from the bow of the barge to about one hundred feet back. They got a barge out of Greenville, Mississippi, to pump the cargo off the grounded barge into. All the boats had got out before they got there with the barge. When the barge arrived, they could not get close enough to the grounded barge to pump it off. They had to leave the barge there for months.

The sounding boat came down and the channel had changed several hundred feet. We waited until a new channel was marked. I don't know how many months that barge sat on a dry sand bar. That barge looked funny sitting on top of a dry sand bar. The barge did not break up, but it was bent out of shape. I was told later on they laid hoses to pump the loaded barge because it had started leaking.

Just above Helena, Arkansas, a northbound tow with all empties hit ground and lost all his barges. The barges hit the bank and the boat tow broke up. One went down the river out in the willow trees on a sand bar. They tried to get it out but finally they gave up until the river came up where a boat could get it.

9. Steamed

Anhydrous ammonia barge

The EPA has done a lot of good at cleaning up the air and water. When I first went in to Pittsburgh on a boat, at night your spotlight was almost useless due to the coal dust. From Wheeling, West Virginia, up the river past Pittsburgh the coal dust was bad. We did not have air conditioning on the boat. When pumping off at Springdale, we would put something over our beds to keep the coal dust off our sheets. After saying this I do think the EPA has taken a lot of things to far that has cost the American people millions of jobs.

***

After I went on the river, we were pumping off at Springdale. I saw the captain and tankerman were setting up the steaming. They had opened the steam on all tanks. I didn't say a thing. It took over four days for the asphalt to get hot enough to start pumping slow. It was taking about thirty days to make two turn-arounds from North Bend, Ohio, to Springdale. The company would have to send another boat up there now and then to catch up. When we got to North Bend, I asked the Captain about putting steam on the barges before we loaded.

"Why?" he asked.

There were two reasons. First, the barges would be hot before we loaded hot asphalt. Next, hot asphalt won't be loading into that cold steel—which doesn't help the steel the barges were made of.

He said, "We don't worry about that."

I shut up.

From the time we started loading until we finished loading, the asphalt temperature dropped about forty degrees.

After we were loaded we headed to Springdale. There we hooked up the steam hose and everybody went to town except the tankerman and me.

We were told the company had a consultant that would be getting on different boats during loading and pumping off. The efficiency expert got on the barges. He was all business and never smiled. He looked down the hatches at a temperature gauge. I called him by his name and asked him to back away from the hatch.

I said, "I am fixing to tell you a joke and when you smile I don't want your face to crack and fall in that asphalt."

He just smiled a little and said, "Henry, I have checked up on you. You done a lot of steaming for a refinery in Houston, which is partly owned by the man you worked for. What are we doing wrong?'

"I'm not the Captain. I'm just watching the circus"

"That's not what I asked." He left and returned a few minutes later. "Where's the Captain?"

"They've gone to town. He's supposed to call the office. I have no idea where he is."

"There's a man on his way up here from the office. If I'm not back when he gets here, call me at my motel."

I told the tankerman I would watch the barge if he would see if he could find the Captain and tell him to call the office. I had gone to bed when the Captain came in about 2 AM He woke me up and wanted to know what the office wanted.

"I have no idea," I told him.

He'd been gone long enough for a person from the office to fly from New Orleans to Pittsburgh and get a car and drive to the docks. He got to the boat about fifteen minutes after the Captain woke me up. The consultant was back as well.

The man from the office, the Captain and consultant were talking and sent a deckhand after me. It was about three, or four in the morning.

The consultant said, "It's your baby don't let it die on you."

"What are talking about?"

I looked at my boss and he said, "Yes, and you are the Captain."

"So, it's my job to see that the steaming and pumping goes right? I didn't come on here to take someone else job, because this is just my second trip and I'm as lost as a dying calf in a hail storm."

"You didn't get his job. He lost it. We will get somebody to stand watch with you southbound a couple trips, if you can make it northbound."

I said, "We'll see."

The man from the office said, "Call me about twenty-four hours before you are pumped off."

I learned on my first trip how to get in the locks southbound. I got the tankerman and told him what we were going to do on the steaming. He didn't like it. We turned all the steam off except number ones. Little over two days we were ready to pump.

About twenty-four hours before we got pumped off I called the man in the office. I asked if he could put the trip pilot on stand-by.

"Why?"

"I would like to try it myself if it's alright."

The office boss said, "That'll be fine, but if you need the pilot call me."

I had one little problem. I had trouble getting in one lock. No damage.

When we got back to North Bend, I got off. My relief wasn't there. I told the dock man we want to heat the barge before we loaded. We connected the steam hose and got the barge hot then started loading. When loading you load the stern tanks first. We put all the steam on the stern tanks. By the time the tanks were inspected and cargo hose connected up, the back tanks were ready to load. We moved our steam to the next tanks. Every tank was hot before the asphalt was put in them. I got off and went home.

After I made it home, the captain called and that relieved me. He wanted to know how we were to steam the barges now. I explained the way it *should be* done, but he was the Captain and he could do it however he wanted.

"The consultant said to call you."

We cut three days off steaming and pumping time the first couple or three trips. Before the summer was over we had increased our trip time from two trips a month to a trip ever nine or ten days. It depended on lock delay.

The consultant was to stay with the company two years. He and I became real good friends. I helped him a lot with barges. After we left the company, he called and wanted to know if I wanted to learn something besides boats and barges. Of course, I did! Over the next few years, he helped with other things.

***

I was the pilot on the boat. A tankerman and I got into a steaming contest. We were at Wood River, Illinois. There were two barges just a like, side-by-side. I told him while we were steaming don't ask me any questions and I won't ask him any, until we've finished steaming and pumping. I was watching the temperature gauges. I went up on the dock to tell the dock man I would be ready to pump by the time they got the discharge hose hooked up. I started the pump engine and let it warm up.

When the docks got the hoses connected, I started pumping. The tankerman and I watched one other, but not a word was said. I'd started on number two tanks when one was about half-pumped. I was stripping my last tanks before his barge was ready to pump. He had been hauling asphalt for years and he couldn't believe what he just witnessed. I explained how to steam a barge.

He quit the boats and went to Chicago, Illinois. He acquired a barge steaming and tankerman's job for an oil company. I saw him years later. He told me he never mentioned to anyone how he steamed a barge. He didn't want any competition.

QUITTING

We had heavy oil to pump off at Norco, Louisiana. It had to be steamed. They had taken and put me on this boat as pilot. I walked out on the barges and notice they had the steam set up their old way.

I said, "You are steaming this barge the wrong way."

Mr. So & So told us to go back to the old way of steaming. This Mr. So & So was another Vice President in the company. This man did not like the consultant. I had a feeling when the consultant left I wouldn't be far behind him, because he had upset some of their apple carts, Also, they found out the consultant was the reason I was with the company. I didn't know this until I'd left. It had crossed my mind about leaving right then. I've walked off of three boats. I was sick and needed to go to the doctor. The owner told anybody with any sense knew doctors didn't work on Sunday.

I said, "You are so stupid, how do you even know it is Sunday?"

I quit then and there before he had a chance to fire me. Another time, I told the owner I needed off by a certain date. That day came and no relief. I got off in Morgan's City, Louisiana. I don't count this because the owner didn't stand up to his end of the deal.

***

I'd been gone three or four months when the vice president of the company that brought my bonus check to North Bend, Ohio, called me. I'd come home off the boat.

"I want to talk to you and then our accountant wants to talk to you," he said. "The company owner wants you to come back to work for him."

"I can't," I answered.

I talked to the accountant and he had the same story. He said, "The owner wants you to come to New Orleans to see him. We'll pay you three days' pay and all expenses."

"What does he want?"

"Why don't you come over and talk to him about it?"

"When does he want me to come?"

"Anytime this week," he said.

"Have me a plane ticket for in the morning from Houston."

He called back. "Is 7:00 AM too early for you to get up and drive to Houston and catch an early morning flight?"

I said, "That'll be fine." I was hoping to get it over with that day.

When I arrived in New Orleans, I was picked up at the airport and taken to the office. The owner was waiting on me. We talked a while and then drove over to Avondale Shipyard to look at a barge. He asked me for my opinion on a couple things; we had lunch and then back to the office.

He said, "I want you to come back to work for us and not working on the boats. I want you to see that my people are steaming the barges correctly. Since you and the efficiency man left, our steaming time has gone up on some of our boat tows. There will be a lot of traveling."

"I gave you my opinion on that barge, so I will give my opinion now. First, nearly all of your people are set in their ways. There is no changing them. Second, I would have to fire over half your tankermen. Third, when I wasn't around they would do it the way they wanted. If you want I can write down how to steam a barge, then have a tankermen and Captain's meeting and you tell them this is the way steaming our barges is going to be steamed."

He said, "So, you want take the job."

I said, "No, I don't."

"I want you to explain to me the best way to steam a barge. I will try to the best of my ability the way you steam a barge," he said.

"You are not going to pump the whole barge at one time so why do you want all the tanks getting hot? It's not only the steam that is heating; it is the pressure on the steam coils that does most of the heating. You are going to pump number one tanks first. Put all your steam on number one tanks. When you get pure steam on number-ones, open number-two tanks a little, but just enough to start blowing the water out of the lines. Cut back on number one's steam out discharge, but not enough to take the pressure off number one lines, but keep the water blowed out. When you get number ones hot enough to pump the more oil you pump out of number one tanks the less steam it is going to take for number ones," I explained.

I continued, "You put more steam on two. Two's will be ready to start pumping before you get ones pumped out, so you start pumping number two's. In most cases two's will be ready to pump before ones are half pumped off. You have already got steam on three. Go right down the line until all tanks are pumped."

"Henry, I know nothing about steaming and pumping barges. I fell into this business by accident. I got people around me to help me get started. This contract came up and I knew nothing about bidding on a job like this. I hired a man from a brokerage firm. He got the contract for me and I didn't have the barges. I didn't have the boats for this job either. Where was I going to get the barges? I hired the accountant I have now and he had boat and barge experience. He found a bank that would loan us the money to build the barges we needed, if we put the contract up for security. We built the barges we needed. The bank wanted to put one of their men with the company for two years," he said.

The man explained more, "When all this came about we had the barges and boats to handle what we had been hauling at the time. The boats we had really wasn't what we needed for this contract. The barges were out of date for this job and not good enough some didn't have steam coils. I bare boat chartered two more boats with the option to purchase. Our first check the accountant got on a train went to Cincinnati picked up the check, because we didn't want to take a chance on the mail, because we needed the money bad. You said just steam going through a line won't heat."

I said, "It will heat some, but you want get the most out the steam; you need pressure steam to heat. It will heat a little, but nothing like if there is pressure on the line. The old man taught me how to steam by showing me. We had pure steam coming out of two lines. We had some temperature gauges with pig tails on them (pig tails on a temperature gage is what you put a liquid to tell the temperature). He wrapped one on each line. He put pressure on one line and left the other open. He left them about an hour. The one that had pressure was almost a hundred degrees hotter than the one with no pressure. I think one of those gauges was wrong. He unwrapped and exchanged them."

I told him all the new barges had steam traps. The purpose of this is to let water out until you get steam coming out. Beside the steam trap, there is a bleed off valve. If you see nothing but water coming out of the steam trap, you open the bleed off valve until you get steam.

He said, "This past winter we had a number of coils to freeze."

I said, "The lines weren't blown out."

He asked, "What if you don't have air?"

"You use steam." I explained how to do this, which is very simple if you know how and keep steam from going back in to the lines you have already blown.

I was hoping to knock this out in one day. Five days from the time I left home, I got back. When I left New Orleans, the old man either knew a lot more, or was more confused. The accountant brought me a check and I didn't look at it until I got on the plane. It was for two weeks. He did call for my help twice.

I wasn't planning on being gone but one day. I drove my wife's car to Houston and she was out of a car for five days. Sometime later one of the Vice Presidents of the company called me. We just had a Captain and tankerman meeting. The owner laid the law down to them on steaming barges.

It was just like you told me, but he wouldn't pay any attention to me because I have never steamed a barge. He asked me to call you to ask if you could come up with steaming report sheet. We have come up with one, but we aren't satisfied with it."

I said, "I'll see what I can do." I must have drawn up two dozen before I came up with one I was satisfied with. They were sent to the office, then out to the boats, then as soon as they could be mailed to the office after steaming a barge or barges they were mailed. As soon as they got to the office the owner would look them over. He would compare barges that were just a like and look at their steaming. He had three big boat tows just alike. He would compare the ones that had the same type cargo. The third boat tow out of four barge boat tow was different. The owner didn't tell me he checked these reports himself, but the Vice President did.

About a year after I mailed the steaming report sheets and the owner called me. "Henry, do you have time next week to go to Chicago for a couple days. I don't want anybody including the people in the office to know about this. I got this one boat tow that it is taking too long to steam for some reason. I need someone to check up on it for me. Some of my people have checked it out and they can't find the problem."

I said, "Call me about a day before it gets to the dock. I am working in the Port Arthur, Beaumont and Lake Charles area doing some shore work, so I can go anytime, within the next month for a couple days."

I got me a pair of horn-rimmed glasses, a wig, tried to change my voice, got a tight-legged suit, a briefcase. There were people on this boat that knew me. These people were one of the main reason I had quit the company any way. This captain was set in his ways.

From the time they docked, I watched them. It took way too long to get the steam lines hooked up. After they had been steaming for a couple hours, I went down onto the barges. I didn't know the tankerman. I told him I was from the insurance company and had to look the barges over. Just what I thought. They were steaming their old way. They were putting steam on all tanks on five barges. I wrote this down as I went. I was up on the dock getting all my notes together when I looked up and the company owner was there looking at me. He said, "Is that you Henry? It is."

He had on some old work clothes. We went down on the barge he said a few words to the tankerman. I let him do the talking or questions. We would pass something and he would say, "That's not right."

"You're correct, it's not."

We went over the five barges then back up on the dock. One thing that got to him was that the Captain, or Pilot, never came out too see who was on the barges. He told me to go on home and he'd mail a check. He said, "I am going to stay and shake things up. I'm not going to let the Port Captain do it, I am."

I said, "That's a good idea."

Port Captain was one of the old-timers. He said, "I'm going to my motel room and put my dress clothes on and come back down here."

I found out later that he had fired some people, including the Captain.

10. Opportunities

MONEY

When I was the regular captain, the Vice President told me, "Henry, there is no way we can make money out of this run; we just do the best we can."

We had to take this run to get the big contracts, which were four big boat tows. I asked if we turn this into a paying deal, will I get a bonus like the captains on the big boats do.

"You sure will and you will have earned it."

The Vice President came to North Bend, Ohio, from New Orleans with the check. It was sixteen hundred and some dollars. I ask him could he get it cashed somewhere. I said to get one's five's ten's and twenties. I kept thirty percent in order to pay taxes on the check, then I split the rest with other crew members. Each man got close to eighty dollars and that included the ones that were on their time off.

***

At one point, when I called my wife, she said two companies called and wanted to talk to me. Turns out, one had a better deal, so I went to work for him. I requested thirty days off to allow me to give two-weeks' notice and have two weeks off. He agreed. I called the man that told the tankerman to go back to their old way of steaming. I told him I would be leaving when we got back south. He agreed and he seemed happy to see me go. These people had been extra good to me and I really hated to leave, but I knew there were too many people against me. The Owner and the Vice President that brought my check to North Bend had been extra good to me.

***

I'd been working as a Captain for a few years and I became tired of running the river and wanted a break. I quit and got me a decking job in the Houston harbor. I'd always enjoyed decking as long as it wasn't too cold.

A man called me about going Captain on one of his boats. I told him I was going to deck for a while in the Houston Harbor for about sixty or ninety days then I'd go back to the river. The next day he called and said he had a decking job.

"When do I start?"

"Be at Charlie Jones' cafe at seven in the morning."

I was there when he arrived.

He said, "Henry, I want you to go to the Illinois River."

I said, "Jack, I don't want to go up there."

He said, "If you'll go, I'll pay a little extra for decking."

I reconsidered. "I'll go on one condition—the people on the boat don't need to know that I'd ever worked on a boat before. I want to enjoy showing people how stupid I can act."

PLAYING THE FOOL

I went to Chicago, Illinois, to get on the boat. The boat was on a regular run from Chicago to Wood River, Illinois. I would get everything backwards. The mate would send me after something. I would bring two different things, telling him I didn't remember which was which.

The mate asked, "How old are you?" I told him.

I could hear remarks being made about how stupid I was.

He said, "How can a man get as stupid as you are in that many years? The Captain doesn't want to fire you, but he is scared you are going to get hurt, why don't you just quit."

"I've got to work to feed a wife and four kids." (I was divorced and had one son.)

Things had been going my way for about fifteen days. We were locking up at Marseilles locks on the Illinois River. A new engineer was getting on at the lock. When he got on the boat he went to the pilot-house. He looked out on the tow and saw me.

"Isn't that Henry Elliott out there on the boat tow?" he asked.

The Captain answered, "Yes, and one of the most stupid people I ever saw. He has been on the boat about fifteen days and he has not learned one thing except meal time."

The engineer started laughing.

The Captain asked, "What's so funny?"

"Well, Captain it is like this. Henry and I got off a boat about thirty days ago where he was the Captain and I was Chief Engineer. We were running from Houston to Pittsburgh.

The Captain commented, "That stupid so-n-so."

I'd left my suitcase on my bed open not thinking. My pilot licenses were where they could be seen.

A deckhand got my license to show the Captain about the time the engineer had finished telling the Captain about me. When we started back to the boat, the Captain said over the PA system for me to come to the pilot-house. One man remarked, "Henry I would pack my bags, because when we get to Chicago, the Captain is going to let you go."

In the pilot-house, the Captain said, "You've made a fool out of us all. Here you drive this thing a while." Jim, the engineer, was hiding and I hadn't seen him.

I said, "Captain, I don't know what you are talking about."

About that time, Jim stood up and I knew the cat was out of the bag. I took the controls and went just a short distant when a deckhand walked in. When he saw that I had controls he went down stairs hollering, "The Captain has let the crazy *b*... drive the boat!"

The Captain had to get off for some reason; Jack called and wanted to know if I would run as Captain until my time was up.

The men on the boat wouldn't talk to me. In fact, they wouldn't come to the pilot-house unless I called them. When we were at the table no one said a thing unless it was me. I passed the word around that when we get to Chicago I wanted to talk to the crew.

We when arrived in the windy city, I brought everybody together. I told them I don't think a thing about all the things they had said about me because I had planned it that way. Jim and I just quit off a boat—you could fit this boat in the engine room of the other boat. I just wanted a rest out of the pilot-house a while and a change.

Now, when I get off, if Jack doesn't have a decking job for me in Houston, I'll find somebody that does."

Jack passed the word around and I had a decking job in Houston before I left Illinois. I worked in the Houston Harbor about sixty days then I went back out on the river.

***

Everybody on the boat got constipated for some reason. We were about to order groceries. I told the cook to make out a laxative list when she made the grocery order.

When I got to the laxative list I got tickled and told the lady who took my order I would have to call her back. I called her back in a little while and finished the rest of the order. I asked for one more thing. "Send me about a dozen cork stoppers."

"What size?" she asked.

"Different sizes."

"Do you want the ones with that are plain with a string, wire or chain?"

I said, "Plain will be fine." She got tickled.

When we arrived in Memphis, they brought our groceries out to us. In the bag were the stoppers. They brought one to the pilot-house with my name on it. It was about two inches in diameter and had a piece of small chain screwed to it. I was off watch when they came. The next day I called the lady and told her she did well, all the corks were a perfect fit.

11. Tomfoolery

OOPSY-DAISY

We were going up the Ohio River and the fog rolled in. Our radar was out and the river was high—out of the banks in some places. Coming up on watch, the captain told me to just nose into the shore and get a line to a tree. I ask the deckhand that was on the bow if he could see a dock or anything that I could hit.

"I don't see a thing," he said then yelled over the PA system, "You just hit a house and there are people in it."

My nerves were a bit shaken and I backed down river a couple miles, to hole up until the fog cleared. When the air was cleared the captain got us underway. As we passed by, I saw how much damage I did to the house. It tore the porch off. When we got to next lock, the captain and I talked to our boss and told him what happened. The boss told us not worry about it. "Let's see if we hear anything."

I don't guess they ever did, because we never heard another word about it.

***

We were northbound with a unit oil tow. The river was high enough to take a few short cuts to get out of the current. If I was running a short cut I would never turn the boat over to the pilot, or Captain, until I was back in the channel. I was going behind an island, but as I started out I felt the barges hit something. I wasn't about to try and stop where I was because I knew I had at least twenty feet of water. I was using my spotlights when I noticed something on the bow barge. When the Captain came up I told him, "I'm going out there and see what it is."

He said jokingly, "It might be an alligator."

It was daylight; I went to the bow barge. Was I surprised when I saw what it was? It was a log that came through our bow air compartment, about eighteen inches in diameter. It was sticking about ten feet above the deck of the barge. I open the hatch cover to see if any water was coming in. There wasn't. I went back to tell the captain. This old Captain had been around a while and he was not surprised. He'd run the Missouri River for years.

We went on up the river to Cincinnati. The log was sticking out below and if we got in shallow water it would drag bottom. When we got to Cincinnati the bow rake didn't have five gallons of water in it. That log was jammed in there tight. We pumped off and went back to New Orleans to reload, but went to the shipyard first and got the log cut out and the holed fixed. This old captain said he had seen a lot of this on the Missouri River.

***

We were hauling oil from Texas City, Texas, to Houston that had to be heated if it just got warm. We had been hauling out of this one refinery for over a month. We were working seven days on and seven days off. When I came back to work I ask the dispatcher what time I needed to be in Texas City. He said, "When you get there."

We got our barge and to Texas City. I pulled up to the dock and got tied off, walked out on the dock. The dock man said, "Well, Henry, what can we do for you?"

"I need 10,000 barrels of Bunker C." They hooked the hose up and started loading. I noticed it was taking a long time to load, but I didn't say anything.

On oil movements to be moved, it had to be released by the refinery, the buyer, and the broker. The hauler would be notified of the releases then they would load the oil. This oil had been released by everybody, but wasn't ready to be moved, which the dock didn't know and my dispatcher didn't tell me because he hadn't been told. I had loaded and was on my way back to Houston when the office called through the marine operator. He wanted to know where I was. I told them about half way between Texas City and Houston. "What is the hold up?" he asked. "The dock is waiting on you."

"I have loaded and am on my way back."

"Where did you load?" he asked and I told him.

"You were supposed to load at American Oil."

I said, "Nobody told the dispatcher I am sure, because he would have told me."

When arrived in Houston, the oil was too cold to pump. They had to make portable steam coils to put in man holes, because the barge didn't have steam coils. It took days to get it pumped off. A man in the office forgot to tell the dispatcher, which saved the dispatcher and me.

***

I was on a small boat coming through Galveston Harbor. We had a long rake barge on a tow line. As I was coming on watch at midnight, I walked up in the pilot-house to look around before I took the wheel.

The Captain said, "I'm over here to stay out of the ship's way while they turn around." We'd passed a ship at anchor on our port, and then about a thousand feet there was another. The Captain said, "When you pass that ship move over to the starboard."

I told the captain I had it. Just as I stepped up to take the wheel, I laid my hand on the wheel and we hit ground. That long rake barge didn't stop until it had shoved the smoke stack down in the engine room, knocking our mask pole and spotlight off the top of the wheel house, plus other damage. I thought we had twenty-five feet of water there, by those ships lying where they were. Everything still worked except our radio and spotlight. We didn't have a muffler.

We started on to Houston with the exhaust discharging in the engine room. We were lucky we had a good wind blowing. You couldn't go in the galley and everybody had to stay on the front deck. We made it to Houston. I knew the captain wouldn't get fired, but I didn't know about Henry. The people from the office came down to inspect the disaster. If it hadn't been for a deckhand in the pilot-house, I would have been fired. He heard the captain talking to the big boss man. When they finished talking the deckhand stopped the boss man when he said, "I know the captain has been with the company since it started, but what he told you would happen is not right."

"Well, why don't we go talk to Henry?" the boss said, "Go get Henry and come to the office." The deckhand had been there for years. All he wanted to be was a deckhand.

He came and got me. We went to the office and went in to see the boss. He said, "Henry, I want to know just what happened in Galveston." I told him word for word what happened, except one thing.

The deckhand said, "Henry you left out something the captain told you."

I said, "Well, he told me that we were in thirty feet of water."

The captain told the boss he was in the galley when we ran aground. I knew as well as everybody else the man that owned the company wasn't going to let this captain be fired.

My oldest brother once told me when I didn't know who I was to relieve, have a witness in the pilot-house when I relieved the pilot on watch.

I made this a practice the rest of my boating career. This practice has saved a lot of discussions.

***

We were tied off just below a bridge on which a lot of people were walking. I looked up in the pilot-house and a deckhand was watching women as they walked across the bridge.

I said, "You had better watch out. You could be looking at a man's wife and he might be with her."

He replied, "They won't come through the gate."

I went downstairs playing rummy when all kinds of noise broke loose from up above. This other deckhand and myself ran to the pilot-house. By the time we arrived, two men had beat the lady watcher up. He spent about ten days in the hospital.

PROBLEM SOLVING

We left Catlettsburg, Kentucky, with a double locking of loads of heavy oil and empties. We had several grades of heavy oil. We were taking them to Baton Rouge, Louisiana, to an oil dock where they'd mix it as we pumped off for fuel for a ship.

When we got to Baton Rouge, the boat owner and his wife got on. It was going to be four or five days before we could get to the dock. We had one empty 25,000-barrel barge you could pump from one tank into another on the same barge. I didn't want to mention this to the owner so I called the office and asked the man in charge of oil movements and asked him why we didn't mix the oil ourselves.

"We can't do that."

I'd mixed oil before, but the refinery always told me where to put a certain kind of oil. The only thing I had to do is make sure we didn't get too much or not enough oil in certain tanks.

We were tied off in a fleet and I thought there was a barge with a boiler on it in the Baton Rouge area. They were about three or four miles away. I went to see the owner. I asked him and his wife if they could come to the pilot-house. I was told we couldn't do it, but with your wife and her slide rule we can.

She asked me where my slide was.

"Home."

I have a calibration sheet on every barge we have in boat tow. We can get a steam boiler on a barge that was in the Baton Rouge area and mix the oil for the ships if the ship broker can give the type of fuel they use. I talked to the ship broker and he gave me the type of oil they needed to burn in their engine. I told the owner to call the oil company and ask how many barrels of this and that to make what the broker gave us. He called the oil company on each barge himself and got all the information we needed.

I said, "Are you all going anywhere before we get this done, because I am going to need your wife and her slide rule." They said no.

The owner said, "What if this doesn't work?"

I said, "You sure got a lot of faith in your wife and me getting this done, but in case it doesn't, you will have 20,000 barrels of oil nobody wants and Henry Elliott out of a job."

I told the slide rule expert I wanted a triple check on everything. When we got it all together, I knew how much oil would be coming out of each tank and how much I would have in the other barge. I forgot how long it took to mix the oil. It took a day or better, because I had been up the whole time. When we finished up the inspectors came out and got samples out of each tank. If you are in the ninety-five percent range it was great. I met the inspector when he came back. He said nine tanks were ninety-nine and some percentage correct and one was ninety-eight. I got the sheet and found the owner, looking as sad as I could.

I had told him if we were in the ninety-five percent range that is almost perfect. He told me to call the boat store ask would they come and get him. He took the sheet with him. To my knowledge that barge never got out of the Baton Rouge and New Orleans area again because it was being used to mix oil. It cut down the delays every trip. I didn't mix any more, and was told they hired a man to mix the oil.

The oil was on the ship as their fuel and we were well on our way to Houston before the dock came open in Baton Rouge. It upset the marine superintendent and he started riding me. I called his name and said he was mad because he didn't think of the idea and he was just a yes man for the oil movement.

"I tell you what to do, get somebody to take my place as soon as possible," I said.

When the owner found out I quit, he called me to find out why. I wouldn't tell him the reason. I just said it was time for me to move on. He wanted me to come and talk to him. I knew what he wanted, but I went anyway, knowing I wouldn't take the job. He got me a round-trip plane ticket and I went to talk to him. He wanted me to come back to work for him. The job was what I thought it was for, but I would have to move. Nobody got me to move from East Texas yet, so why should I start now? A major oil company had offered me a Vice President position in their inland marine department at the age of twenty-eight, but I would have to move and I wasn't moving. Why should I move now? I knew where the good catfish fishing holes were and where the good hunting was.

***

A boat owner called me to see if I would go to Paducah, Kentucky, to get on a boat for a few days while he rounded up a crew. He had fired everyone. I rented a car, drove to Paducah, and got on the boat. When I arrived, a generator was running. I checked the other generator, started it and shut the other one down. I went to sleep and something blew up under my bed. It scared me and I ran outside. The odor gave it away. We found twenty-seven bottles of raisins jack—a home brewed alcohol.

12. Shenanigans

We had a cook and maid on the boat. The maid helped the cook, cleaned the Captain's and pilot's room plus the engineer and did the boat laundry. She had one of those rolling irons she used on the sheets. She would fold the sheet, put the sheet in the iron, and pull the arm down on the sheet so it would pull the sheet through ironed.

I spent two months trying figure out how to make the iron run backwards. I knew how I could do it, but would require some fast changing. I finally had it down and I had practiced a number of times before trying it.

It was her day to iron the sheets, which she did after supper. I changed the iron so when she put a sheet in, it would kick it out instead of pulling it through. I raised a window a little so I could hear what she was saying. She called the cook to show her what was happening. The cook said maybe it needed turning around. That put the control next to the wall.

"I am going to get that little fat slob because I know he has done something to my iron!" she shouted.

I ran upstairs jumped in bed with clothes and shoes on. She knocked on my door and I made out like I was a sleep.

"I am going up and make the other beds. Then you are going down stairs to show me what you did to my iron!" she yelled through my door.

I jumped out of bed, ran downstairs and changed the iron around like it was supposed to be and went back to my room and pulled off my shoes. She came by and I told her to wait, I would have to put my shoes on. I got my shoes on and went downstairs to the laundry room. She got a sheet and put it in the iron and it pulled it right on through ironed and all. She called the cook in there to witness what the iron had been doing.

I put my arm on her shoulders and then called her name. "You have been on the boat about forty days. I know a doctor in St. Louis that we can…" That was as far as I got.

She jumped out of chair. "I'm not the one that needs a doctor! You do, for doing things like this to me."

She was a great lady; we were always pulling things on each other. One time she brought her grandchildren down to the boat. There were two girls and a younger boy. We were sitting in the galley and I was teasing the kids. The boy was about five. I got him down to one end of the table talking to him.

I said, "You mean to tell me that old gray-headed woman is your grandma."

I said few other things before he got down off the stool, walked around to the other side of the table, crawled up in a chair where he was looking me eye ball to eye ball. He took his finger and put it in my face and said, "No one talks about my Grandma like that and lives to tell about it."

His sisters and his grandma had to to get him settled down. Before he got off the boat he and I were big buddies.

***

I rode this boat with the same maid and cook for about a year and half off.

I was riding pilot and I got off watch at six in the morning. I passed my room on my way to the galley and I noticed a little water right by my door. I ate and set around talked a little. At the top of the stairs, I could go outside and come in my room from the outside. I went in my room from the outside. There was a bucket of water tied over my door, so if I had opened that door out of the hall it would have dumped two gallons of water on my head. I took the bucket down, poured some water under door out into the hall and some on my floor, and then went to bed. I got up about nine and went to the galley.

I said, "Good morning, ladies. How are you all doing?"

"Fine," they said, but the maid wouldn't look me in the eye. Usually when we talked, she never took her eyes off mine. She said that was the only way she could tell if I was lying or not.

I just let the bucket and water pass until I got off and went back to the boat. I went in her room and tied the bucket of water over her door. She got the whole two gallons on her head. She came to the pilot-house and looked like a drowned rat. They wore white uniforms then and usually she was as neat as she could be. I called her by her name said, "What on earth happen to you?"

"Don't you give me that innocent look and try to sweet talk me."

I said, "No, I want to know what happened to you."

"Well, there's a certain fat pilot who tied a bucket water over my door and when I open the door it poured on me."

"That's such a shame for somebody to do you that way," I said.

I was well on my way making her think it was someone else, when a deckhand was coming up the stairs and said the wrong thing, him not knowing the maid was standing right there. There was no doubt in her mind then.

***

I used Listerine as a mouthwash. I had used all the Listerine and just let the bottle set there. When the maid came to clean my bedroom, she broke the top out of her Pine Sol bottle. She saw the Listerine bottle so she poured the pine sol in the Listerine bottle, but forgot and left it in my bath. I got ready to get my afternoon nap I noticed the bottle. I knew I had emptied it so I opened to smell. It was Pine Sol.

I sat by the stairs until I heard somebody coming. I called them in my room and told them what had happened. I put some toothpaste in my mouth to make a foam and then I put some Pine Sol on the outside of my mouth. The deckhands went down and told the maid and cook, "Something's wrong with Henry. He's laying up there on the floor just kicking and foaming at the mouth."

Here they came. "Captain Henry, don't die!"

Somebody said, "He will be dead before we can get him to a doctor."

I got tickled and those two women like to have beat me to death.

***

If we were stopped somewhere, I would look at how the maid set up the table for this one Captain. I noticed she got two half-gallons of milk out of the refrigerator and set them down.

One morning before they got down to fix breakfast, I got a half-gallon carton with just little milk and filled it up with water and put it in the refrigerator. This Captain never smiled or had a kind word for anybody. The maid sat that half-gallon with water by the Captain's plate. I watched through the window. I had no idea what he would say or do, but I knew I would cut in on him if he got on the maid or cook. He poured the milky water and looked at it.

He called the maid and she came in. He said, "What happened to this old cow?"

She looked at it and said, "Well, Captain, I would say Henry milked that one."

He said, "That figures. I want you to get a half-gallon and let it sour good then put it by Henry's plate."

I never took the bait.

***

We had plastic glasses to drink from. They would stack them in a cabinet. One day I started to get a glass of milk and the two glasses stuck together. We were at a dock and right before the cook and maid came down to fix breakfast an idea came to me. I went down and taped them together. You should have seen them trying to get the glasses apart. I was outside watching and I got so tickled I had to move away from the window. I didn't know a person could get in so many positions trying to get two glasses apart.

The same maid smoked Camel cigarettes. There was another person on the boat that smoked Camels. I said to him, "Let me borrow a cartoon and then tell people you got a carton of cigarettes missing."

I got the cartoon of cigarettes and hid them in the maid's room. After the news a carton of cigarettes were missing, I said, "I guess we are going to need to search the rooms."

The maid said, "You can search mine first." The maid's room was last. Everybody saw us search the room.

I found the cartoon of cigarettes over behind her bed. She looked me dead in the eye. "I did not steal any cigarettes."

Everybody on the boat took her side. I was out in the cold. The man I got the cigarettes from told everybody what happened.

I was on watch and when I went down to my room, every stitch of my clothes was in a big garbage can full of water. I went down to the maid and told her I was sorry for what I did; I also said I needed to borrow the washing machine. When I got off watch the next time, she had washed and ironed all my clothes. All too soon, she had to get off the boats to go home and take care of her mother. She was a mother to the whole crew.

***

While on the same boat with a different maid, I got to noticing how the captain and new maid looked at one another; she would go to the pilot-house when he was on watch—every watch. I could tell if the Captain used the outside door when he left his room. With the door open there was a change in the sound of the engines in the pilot-house.

I couldn't see the maid's outside door from the pilot-house. I got me two ropes long enough where I could steer and see the maid's outside door. Sure enough he would go out his outside door and ease down and go in the maid's room.

I figured out how to block the outside door and the one in the hall. I always did things like this by myself because I didn't want it to be known. He usually stayed in her room about an hour. When I heard his door open I got the mate up there to steer for me. I went down and blocked both doors and turned the fire alarm on. You should have seen both the captain and maid trying to come out the window at the same time. After this happened, the Captain was a nice fellow to work with.

***

The Captain usually had his own bathroom or shared with the pilot. I went to make a trip on a boat where the bath was shared by four or five people. I started to take a shower, but before I did, I went to the galley and got me a handful of peanut butter. When I pulled off my shorts, I smeared the peanut butter in the seat. After I got my shower, I just left the shorts laying there.

I went on watch and the deckhand that cleaned the bathroom came to the pilot-house. He said, "Henry, there is a pair of underwear on the bathroom floor and I think they are yours." I said he should just throw them in my room. He said, "I'm not going to mess with them. They've been messed in!"

I said to the mate for him to steer and let me go check. I went down with the deckhand and I walked around the underwear then picked them up. I ran my finger through the peanut butter and tasted of it.

I said, "Yep, they are mine."

He got sick and wouldn't go to the galley if I was in there. From then on, if I walked in the galley and he was in there, he'd leave.

***

One of the cooks would take T-bone steaks out of the freezer for Saturday night. I'd catch her not looking and I'd put them back in the freezer. She did this three or four times. I was in the dining room and she asked, "Henry, I know I've taken those steaks out more than twice."

I said, "Yes, and I was just wondering why you were putting them back."

A couple days later a deckhand came to me, said the cook is getting worried about herself. I ask why. "She keeps talking about getting the steaks out and putting them back," he explained.

I went down to the galley and told her it was me who put the steaks back. She said, 'Thank God, I'm not losing my mind."

I thought that would be the end of it, but it wasn't. About three days later I had to live on the commode and keep a five-gallon can in the pilot-house. After about four days, she said, "Now, put the steaks back in the freezer on me again."

***

We were boat towing lube oil from Houston, Texas, to Gary, Indiana. When we went through Chicago lock and if Lake Michigan was a little rough, we would put the barge on a boat tow cable. One of the men came to me and wanted to know how to keep from getting seasick. The galley was on the back with two portholes to look out the back. I said to stand right there and watch that barge as it swings. In about ten minutes, he threw up everything he had in his stomach. I left the galley and the cook said Henry was just playing a trick on you. When we got to Gary, he was mad. He saw me and called me everything in the book. After that, anything I told him he would go ask somebody else was I telling him the truth.

***

I was pushing some barges that had boilers on them to keep heavy oil hot by doing this we didn't have to steam the barge to get the oil hot when we got to the dock. They needed to be checked every hour or so, day and night. We were sitting on the front of the boat just talking.

I said, "How many believe in ghosts?"

Three or four said that they sure have seen some strange things in their life. On the barges, we had a PA system with speakers that could be moved around. I went on the barges like I was just looking around and I put a speaker in each boiler house. I would bring up ghosts every now and then. We were at "cave in rock" on the Ohio River waiting on a lock fifty.

The engineer went out to check the boilers and when he would start in one, I would make a strange noise. He would back out and go to the door on the other side and I would do the same thing. He went on out to another boiler house the same thing happen.

I noticed the engineer coming back to the boat. He came to the pilot-house and asked if a deckhand could go with him.

I said, "Sure."

They started in the first boiler house when I did the same thing. They backed off, got their flashlights and looked all around. They moved on to the other, then they came back.

"Henry, there is all kinds of strange noises out there."

I said, "Here, I will go with you all. Let me get the mate to watch the boat." We went out there. I said, "I don't hear anything."

They couldn't hear anything so we went back to the boat.

I had got two long springs and made a sling shot. I put it on the barge next to the boat. I got me a white pillowcase and tied a big nut for a bolt in one corner.

The engineer and deckhand were about fifty feet from where I was. I had the pillowcase rolled up around the big nut. I pulled the sling shot back and let it go. That nut was out front and that pillowcase flopping in the wind. I had a hard time beating them back to the pilot-house. The engineer and the deckhand came to the pilot-house to see if I'd seen that ghost. I said, "I can't believe two grown men are seeing ghosts."

***

The engineer and cook were husband and wife. I got to noticing how he watched me and I didn't know why. There wasn't anything pretty about his wife and she was old enough to be my mother. When I was in the galley to eat, the engineer would be there. I could go get a cup of coffee and he would be there. I got to where I would just go to the galley to eat only. I was sitting in the pilot-house, when I mentioned this to a deckhand. He said you don't know why? I said no. One of the deckhands told the engineer he had better watch Henry, or he would steal his wife. I decided I would go along with it.

In the engine room there was a big tank that fuel was pumped into to run the main engines and generators. This tank had an alarm on it so if the fuel got low the alarm would go off. The tank had a big float with a rod sticking out at the top that the engineer could watch just in case the alarm didn't work. I would see the engineer sitting in his chair down in the engine room. I would pass this tank and push this rod down. When I did the alarm would go off and I would go to the galley and get a cup of coffee.

Here came the engineer. He would sit there until I left. I did this a few times when I got to thinking this could get serious. So I quit and just went to the galley to eat.

Later we were getting off the boat and he had his car there. I needed to go to the airport that he passed by so I asked him would he give me a ride to the airport.

He said, "NO! You have been trying to steal my wife ever since you got on the boat and you expect me to give you a ride? You can walk."

A couple days later, I needed to call the office about something. The man I was talking to said, "Henry, what are you doing trying to steal my cook?" And he broke out laughing.

The engineer had told him he wouldn't ever ride a boat with me because I tried to steal his wife. I told him the story of what I had done after I found out what one of the men told the engineer. The owner told me all most every trip pilot that was put on there, it was the same thing.

***

I had a first mate and his wife was the cook on the boat. Some knew they were married and some didn't. I had known them for years. When he knew he would be getting up a lot with the double locking boat tow, he would sleep in the mate's room, if not he would sleep in the cook's room. I sent a deckhand down to get the mate. He went to the mate's room and he wasn't there.

The deckhand came back and said, "He isn't in his room and I can't find him."

I said, "Go down to the cook's room, he may be in there."

He was serious when he said, "Captain Henry, I did not figure you for that type of person, letting the mate sleep with the cook."

I said, "I do things like that now and then."

When he found out they were married, he came to me and said, "You let me make a jackass of myself."

***

I worked for a Captain that was a boxer in his youth. He was called "Punch Happy." He would not stay in the pilot-house at night by himself because he was scared. One night, I decided to have a little fun. I had got a sheet and put it in an air compartment on the barge. When it got dark, I eased out and got in the air tank. When he started using his spotlights I would stick my head up a little then back down. I stuck my head up with the sheet over it. *BOOM, BOOM.* I didn't know he had a shotgun in the pilot-house. I happened to be far enough away that two shots stuck in my scalp.

***

I was working on a boat where the cook and deckhand quarters were in the in the forward hole. There was a hatch cover in the deck above our quarters. There was a fan between our quarters and the engine room. It served two purposes. It sucked air into our quarters to cool them and helped cool the engine-room. The boat was engine-room controlled and the engineer was on the side of the engine where the fan was.

The engineer was leaning back getting a little nap. I got a can of black pepper and put some in the fan. The engineer just wiggled his nose a little. I then gave him a lot. He came up and ran outside to get some air. Nothing was ever said about it. My bunk was right under the hatch cover. The engineer must have dumped a whole box of red pepper in the hatch door. The only way out was up through a door in the floor of the galley. The engineer stood on the door where I couldn't get out. My nose burned for two days.

***

A cook I once worked with griped and complained about everything. On this little boat we would put our suitcases in the engine room, unpack, and store them there. I got a piece of stinking cheese and put in his suitcase. It stayed in that hot engine room two weeks. When he opened his suitcase you could smell it for a hundred yards. He didn't say a thing about it. It aired out a couple hours before he put his clothes in the suitcase. He got off and never said a word. He came back to the boat and I was getting off. I got dressed and started to put my dress shoes on and ran my foot in my shoe into a raw rotten egg. I had to wear my work shoes home.

13. Great Ideas

In the mid-fifties, I saw a small boiler that made steam. It came to me, why can't they put one of those on a barge to keep asphalt hot. I got a few sheets of paper and started drawing plans. I had the water supply tank, the fuel tank, and boiler in a house. I was in New Orleans and I went to the Coast Guard with my drawing. They just said no boilers on oil barges. When I went home, I went to the Coast Guard in Houston Texas. They told me the same thing. I didn't give up.

I knew a retired Coast Guard Commander, but I had no idea where he lived. He had a name I couldn't even pronounce. I just forgot about it then his name came to me. I got another Coast Guard to see if he could find out where he lived. A few months later I found out he lived a few miles from Houston.

I was undecided whether to go ahead or let it drop. About two years after the idea first hit me, I found his phone number and called him. He was interested so I went to Houston and we met for lunch. I'd already made three or four drawings. I gave him one. I didn't hear a thing for a long time. I receive a call to meet with the Coast Guard in Houston at the Coast Guard office. I never answered so many *ifs* in my life.

I located some heavy oil barges being pumped in Houston. These people were not from Houston; rather they were from Washington, DC. I took them down to oil refinery so they could get a picture of what I was talking about.

I said, "I am not talking about anything but asphalt."

One man seemed to like the idea. The other guy wasn't sure. They asked me what the flashpoint on asphalt was and I didn't know. They found out what they wanted to know while we were at the refinery. This was in the late fifties. I never heard another word.

In 1963, I was hauling asphalt. We went to the shipyard. What did they do? Put boilers on those two barges to keep the asphalt hot. There were some restrictions if we hauled other types of oil like setting the boilers off or taking the electronic box off the boiler control panel. Somebody else might have had the same idea before me. I will never know. My idea may have never got past file thirteen. The trashcan.

***

In Louisville, Kentucky, the old dam had wickets (large door or opening built to control water levels). When the river got high enough, they could let down the wickets, so, southbound you didn't have to lock if the river was that high. They would drop the wickets and you could go over the dam. I'd never been through there. The Captain hadn't been through there, either. When we got down to the dam, for about a mile, it was a wild ride. When you went over the dam, you dropped two or three feet. I don't know how the boat and barges stayed together. I promised myself that would never happen again and it didn't. They did away with the wickets and made a fixed dam later.

***

Once when I was the pilot on the boat, the captain came aboard with new pair of work shoes that were too tight on his feet. I told him to lace them up, go to the galley, and fill the shoes up to the lace with pinto beans. Then, I told him to fill his shoes with water to the laces. Lastly, pack rags behind the beans and stand the shoes on their toes. Most importantly, I told him, "Don't leave them over thirty minutes." Well, he forgot them. When he went to get his shoes, one had pulled the top from the sole and the other was big enough to fit both feet in. He should have listened to old Henry!

***

We were coming down the Atchafalaya River where I was running as pilot. We were about to make Simmesport Bridge in Louisiana. My intentions were to drop the barges under a wide span, because the boat wouldn't go under the wide span, back up and run a span that would open with the boat. The span that would open was wide enough for barges and boat. It was about 130 feet wide, but 100 feet wide and 600 feet long it was impossible to make the bridge with the river as high as it was. The kicker was to cross current above the bridge. If you tried to make the bridge at this stage of river, you either hit the bridge, dragged the bridge pier hard, or broke your tow into pieces.

The captain came to the pilot-house and asked my intentions at the bridge. I told him what my plans were.

He said, "You better let me have the controls." So, I stepped out the way.

He stopped above the bridge until the bridge channel span was open. He started easing down to the bridge. I left the pilot-house because I didn't want to witness what was about to happen. I told the mate to make sure everybody was up and their life jackets were on. The captain was lined up perfect to make the bridge until the cross current got the head of the tow.

When I saw what was about to happen, I ran down and closed all the doors on the starboard side. We were about to land crossways of the bridge and I knew the current would be building water up on the starboard side. I broke into a run toward the pilot-house. The Captain was in his chair with his hand frozen to the steering levers. I tried to get them loose. I knew the way the water was piling up on the side it was just a matter of minutes until the boat would sink. I yelled over the PA system for help.

We got the Captain's hands loose and slid him out of the way. I told the mate to cut the wires on the starboard side and run for the inside, because broken cables were about to fly. When the cables broke on the starboard side, I had my rudders hard down to starboard and came full ahead, breaking all the cables on the port side. I figured the bridge was going to get the smoke stacks and part of the upper house. That was better than letting the boat sink. All we lost was our back mask pole and our john boat.

The Captain was still sitting in his chair as white as a sheet. The barges were crossways of the bridge. I got the boat next to the bank to make cable repairs and called the bridge tender to call an ambulance to come to get the captain. I was told to go up river about a thousand feet and the ambulance could come right down to the riverbank. This man was frozen in the position he was sitting in the chair. That is the way they carried him up the hill. The ambulance driver told me he had never seen anything like that before.

I called the company and told them what had happened. I told them the barges were still cross ways of the bridge and I hadn't figured out how to get them yet. I would figure out something. He said, "I will have another pilot at Melville Bridge."

The mate told me they had all the cables replaced on the winches. I came up with a plan, but I didn't know if it would work. I called the mate to the pilot-house and gave him my plan. He had a better one—the best idea I'd heard of and if it didn't work we'd all go to the house.

I went below the bridge and eased up to the barges next to a bridge pier. There was a four-part rope around the bridge pier that rose about fifty feet where it could be connected to the barge. We needed to pull the barges down about seventy-five feet to the next bridge pier. Things didn't go as smoothly as I hoped, but it worked. I went down on one end of the barges and put out several ropes between the boat and barges and started backing slow. One barge had a strong current on one side and I wasn't sure I could pull it up against the current without breaking the cables or pulling the deck fittings out of the barges. I just kept giving it a little more fuel, when the mate said, "We are moving." From the time it started moving until the barges were clear of the bridge only took about five minutes. This all started about 2 PM and at 4 AM the next morning the cables were put between the boat and barges. Everybody had been up so I stopped about four hours for a little rest and gave the office time to round up a pilot and get him to Melville Bridge.

I'd called the Captain at home two or three times and he wouldn't talk to me. I was told the company also tried to call him and he wouldn't talk to them either. I don't think he ever came back to the river.

***

After working in the office, I did two other businesses, and one earned more money than I ever hope to earn. Later, when I went back to the boats, I had decided I didn't want to take any more captain jobs. I just wanted to stand my watch, get the boat up and down the river, get off watch, go to bed and forget everything.

Back on the boats, we were coming out of the upper river just above Cairo, when the engineer came and woke me up. He said, "There is something wrong with the Captain."

I put my clothes on, went to the pilot-house. I sat down on the couch and the captain started cussing that he couldn't find his medicine. He was a nervous wreck; he couldn't talk or stand up.

We were about to make the last bridge out of the Upper Mississippi at Cairo. I said, "Captain, can I help you in any way?"

"Take these d--- controls." He had already gotten the boat tow in such shape to make the bridge that I didn't want it, but I took the controls and got through the bridge. He said, "Call a harbor boat to come and get me and put me a shore."

I never heard from him again. A few years before I had

worked with him and he was a great Captain to work under. I don't know, but I think he was taking the little pills. A bottle of pills was found in his room with no name on it. I got one of the pills and brought it home for my doctor to tell me what it was. The doctor said it was to settle your nerves. I may be wrong, when this captain didn't have something to settle his nerves he went all to pieces.

I called the company to send a captain and told them what happened. You take the captain's job because I am sending a pilot.

I said, "When he gets off, send a captain."

The only reason I liked the captain job was the 6-12 shift. The midnight-to-six watch was really hard on me from about two to four.

14. The Proper Authorities

COAST GUARD

We had an oil barge with papers that were about to expire. The company told me that the Coast Guard was going to get on and do an inspection on the fly until the barge was unloaded. This wasn't unusual.

An inspector and a higher ranking officer got on at Memphis, but I found out this high ranking officer wasn't from Memphis. The inspector checked the barge over, and then told me some things that were going to need to be done that were new. I ask him if he would pass it on to my office and he said he would.

The man with all the braids on his hat asked if he could ride to Cairo with us if we had room. I said, yes and had the guest room fixed up for him. He never went to bed on the trip. He would go lay down a little while, but spent most of the time in the pilot-house. When he got on, he had a little bag. He had some plain old work clothes he put on. He talked to me and the pilot a lot. He went down in the engine room and talked to the engineers, but when mealtime came, he was the first one to the table.

He and I got to talking about regulations. He said, "You just don't know what's coming. I won't see it because I have less than a year to go then I am gone. In fact, I can go now, but I got a project that I started and I want to finish it's. It taking longer than I figured it would. What did you do the last time you renewed your license?"

"I don't remember if it was required, but I got a physical from my family doctor and took it with me. I took my license to the Coast Guard. They told me I would have to wait until license department got back from lunch. If I am not mistaken by 2 PM—I had my new license and was on my way home."

He said, "Those days will be over before too long. Something else they are giving the Coast Guard too much power over things they know nothing about. Look at this. The Engineers have sounded this river for years. These are people that know this river. Most of the Corps of Engineers were born and raised on or around the river. I was in Washington and heard they are about to turn that over to the Coast Guard. The Coast Guard doesn't need that. Leave it to the experts. They will put somebody down here from the east coast that didn't know there was a Mississippi River until they got to it."

He knew what he was talking about, I read about it all time.

***

My brother and I were southbound with a three-barge boat tow. The bow barge exploded just as we were going over the pass at lock fifty-one. It killed one man. There was floating ice in the river. A deckhand went up to turn the boat loose from the barges. He couldn't so he went to the back and jumped in the river with ice and all. There was another boat in the area that helped us tie the barges off. Just one barge caught fire. When the fire was put out we got the barges together.

Before we moved anything or anybody went home, the Coast Guard had a hearing at lock fifty-one. They talked to everybody. The commander asked the man that jumped from the stern him how long it took him to swim to the shore.

"It didn't take long. I swam up beside a boat with fifty horsepower engine and told the man if he was going to beat him to the shore he had better come on."

The commander said, "After that it's time for coffee."

Everybody had to give a written statement. Another

company boat arrived to assist, I had to get off and go home. This is the first and last time in my boating career that I felt like I didn't need to handle a boat tow. In fact, I think the whole crew was changed out.

***

I had an accident in the canal and it wasn't my fault. The Coast Guard tried to make it look like it was my fault and if they could have proven this, they would have taken my pilot license. This was before they changed the name of the license. Back then you didn't need a license unless it was a steam boat. I don't know how many days I was in court. I asked my lawyer if I could say something to the Coast Guard lawyer. He said okay. All I wanted to do was make him mad and say something to me, and he did that. The Coast Guard shouldn't have said a thing to me unless I was on the stand. The first question my lawyer asked me ended the hearing. I told my lawyer what the Coast Guard lawyer told me. My lawyer asked me was there any Coast Guard present that told me as long as I had those license he would reach and get me any time he wanted me. I said, yes sir. The three hearing officers got their heads together about two minutes and the officer in charge said all charges are dropped. End of hearing.

***

The company had an oil barge on dry dock for a Coast Guard inspection. (I was working in the office at this time). I left the office so I could be there at 10 AM where I was to meet the Coast Guard. He went over the barge with a fine tooth comb. Lunchtime came I asked the Coast Guard officer to eat with us.

He weighted maybe 140 lbs and was about 5'4" tall. He ate a T-bone steak, an order of shrimp, and two big pieces of cake. I could not believe what the man ate.

I was even more surprised when he handed me the report of the repairs he was requiring. I asked him how many barges had he inspected. I knew he hadn't done many, because he had his book with him. I told him some of the stuff he had on there was not required on inland barges. I took the report back to my boss. I said, "You could build a new barge if you got to do all the things he wants done to the barge. I told him a lot of the things he had marked were for sea going barges." I said, "Call Commander so & so, or I will.

He said, "I will take care of it."

He called the Commander. The Commander told my boss for Henry to be there in two hours. I was there and there was an older inspector and the one that inspected the barge the first time.

He said, "How are you doing, Henry?"

I said, "Fine. You?"

"I am going to be transferred to the northeast coast in a couple months."

"Who is going to take your place?"

He pointed to the new inspector. "By the time I leave, he will be okay. He will be with me the next forty five-days."

The new inspector turned out to be all right when he learned a sea-going barge from an inland barge.

CORPS OF ENGINEERS

Before they started putting rock dikes on the lower Mississippi, the channel could change in a couple hours. The Corps of Engineers had a survey boat marking the channel; I was following a unit tow, to make a crossing. The boat I was following was following the survey boat. A contact pilot for the Engineers out of Memphis was on the boat ahead of us. They bumped bottom a couple times, but they made it. The contact pilot called me and told me not try until the survey boat had a chance to sound again. I was waiting when the pilot came on watch. I told him to hold up until the survey boat had a chance to sound the crossing again. The survey boat couldn't even come back the way they went. He had been gone a couple hours. We waited over two days for a dredge to get there. Then we had to wait for them to dredge us a channel.

GAME WARDENS

This is one of the times I left the river a couple months. I was hauling gas from Corpus Christi to Brownsville, Texas. Back then you didn't worry about the Coast Guard. It was the Game Wardens. If they caught you with a barge leaking, you went right to jail. The fine was $125 cash. It made no difference who was on watch; the captain was the one that went to jail.

They pulled me off at Port Isbell, Texas. The money had to come out of Corpus. By the time the money got there, the money takers had done gone home. I spent the night in jail. They wouldn't let you pay the Game Warden's office in Corpus. After that, I made sure I always had $125 cash on me!

***

We were hauling asphalt in to Eddyville, Kentucky. About a mile above the dock, a tree had fallen off a bluff into the river. I got the outboard and went up there to see if I might catch a few fish. No luck. When I got off the boat I went home and when I got ready to go back to the boat, I took me a sack of fish bait.

As soon as we got to Eddyville, I took my sack of bait and dropped it in the tree top. The next day I went up and caught fish until I was tired. A little boat with an older fellow came up. I caught three while he was asking a question. He looked in my boat and said, "I think you're over the limit."

I said I didn't know what the limit was. He pulled out his billfold; he was a Game Warden.

"You got any licenses."

I said, no sir.

He said, "What you are going to do with over the limit?"

I figured with no license they were all over the limit. I said, "You can have them all if you want them."

He said, "I don't want them all."

I said, "Let's go down to the boat."

We took our boats and went down to the boat I worked on. We went in the galley and asked the cook if she wanted some fish. She didn't want to clean them so I told the Game Warden to take them all and got him a sack to put the fish in.

He said, "Give me ten dollars and a Kentucky address and I will have you some fishing licenses."

When I got back up there, he had my license. After that, I never went back to Eddyville again.

***

U.S. MARSHALLS

Over the years, of all the companies I worked for, I was never fired, or laid off but one time when a U.S. Marshall tied the boat up. Back then if the Marshall tied a boat up and you were appointed by the Marshall to stay on the boat you had better stay there. I slipped off and when I got off the plane in Houston, Texas, they were waiting for me. They put me back on a plane back to New Orleans. The pay was five dollars a day. The man that owned the boat paid me a little out of his pocket. I finally talked the Marshall into letting me off. The boat was tied off at Avondale Shipyard in Harvey, Louisiana.

My brother was on a boat that I found out the Marshalls were waiting for in Morgan City, Louisiana, to tie the boat up. He was coming down the Atchafalaya River, Louisiana, and I called and told him. He got the pilot up and my brother got off on the swing bridge in Morgan's City. The Marshalls got on the boat about a mile below the bridge and tied it up. They had appointed an engineer to stay on the boat. He was on there for a long time. I was told he got his wife to come and stay with him.

Breaking ice on Illinois River with barges

15. Frozen

We were working on the upper Mississippi and temperature was about zero. I turned the heater on in the bathroom and that's where I left my clothes. I piled blankets and quilts from my bed, then open the outside door, and turned the heat off in my room. I woke up one morning and there was about a foot of snow in my room by the door.

One particular morning it was well below freezing in my room. I jumped and ran to the bathroom where it was warm. While I was on watch my bathroom window was unlocked. Usually, the heater was right under the window. The heater had been turned off, the window was raised and there was ice in the commode. By the time I was dressed I felt like I had ice in me. I went on to the galley to eat breakfast as if everything was normal. After this event, I cut a stick to put over the window where it couldn't be raised. I made sure it was in place before I went to bed.

***

I called the train depot in Conroe, Texas, to see if the trains were running into Memphis. They told me they were so I made my way to Conroe and got on the train. Everything went fine until we got below Little Rock and snow started building up on the tracks. We made it into Little Rock. They put on a couple more engines and added a bunch of old cars that had coal-burning heaters in them. The snow had built up on the tracks and we were out of coal. I took all my extra clothes and let a man's wife and two small children have them except what I had on.

We had to stop for them to clear the tracks. I looked out the window and there was a lot of wood stacked on a porch. I found the conductor to ask how long we would be there. It will be an hour or so. I got a man to go with me and we went and knocked on the door. An older black man came to the door. I ask him if he would sell me some wood.

He said, "No, it's too cold to get any more."

"I'll give you ten dollars for that stack."

He sold it to me. We loaded up and took it to our car. There was about one more load. I told the man to sit on that wood and don't move because somebody would steal it. He got a fire started while I went after the rest. There were four or five children in this car. I ask their parents would they let them come by the heater. They all agreed. We built just a small fire to try and make it last. People from other cars would try to steal the wood.

We finally made it to Memphis. The conductor gave an address and a note. I sent this note to this address, and I got my ten dollars back.

I figured I would have to go above Memphis to get on the boat. The ice coming down the river had moved all buoys off station and the boat was between Helena, Arkansas, and Memphis. I had to wait on the boat after all. The boat store had some bunks and I found me one. I'd been up about forty-eight hours.

***

There was an ice gorge about ten miles above Cairo on the upper river. I have no idea how many boat tows were tied up below Cairo on the Mississippi and on the Ohio River above Cairo. Four or five boats including the boat I worked on went up to check the gorge. When we got there, we saw the difference in the water level above the gorge and below. I asked the captain if they were going to try to break the gorge.

He said, "We might."

I said, "If you decide to, get where I can get on the bank, because you know what's going to happen when it breaks." They decided not to try it. I was in a small gorge a year before when it broke. We were just helpless with the horsepower we had then.

***

We were going up the Allegheny River and there was floating ice in the river and the men were on the barges working. One of the men ran to the pilot-house said, "Somebody is out there hollering for help."

I took my spotlight and started looking. There was some ice frozen to a bridge pier and a person hanging on to it. The mate put a lifejacket on, tied a rope around himself, and jumped in the river. The crew pulled them up on the barge. It was a woman and when her hair hit the barge it froze to the barge. They had to cut her hair off. The crew got her inside and wrapped her in blankets while I called the police. I went on up river to a dock where she could be taken off. She had got to where she could talk, but didn't know her name or where she lived. They got her in an ambulance and we went on up the river. From what we could find out later she had escaped from a women's institution upriver.

***

I was asked by the company I worked for if I would help another company out of a bind. If I'd known what bind they were in, I might not have gone.

I went up on the Ohio River and it was frozen solid. We were between old locks fifty and fifty-one. We were sitting still when a deckhand came and woke me up; in fact the boat had not moved since I got on.

He said, "We got a leak."

I got up and went down to look. They had three or four pumps, but they had them sitting outside in zero degree weather. You had to go through the galley to the front deck storage where the leak was.

I said, "Captain, are you going to sit here and let the boat sink?"

"I don't know what to do," he responded.

I said, "Do you want it to sink?"

He said again, "I don't know what to do."

"You tell these people to take orders from me then you go to your room, or you can let it sink," I told him. "Move those pumps into the galley."

The cook said, "You are not going to put those old pumps in here."

I told her to keep her mouth shut or go to her room.

She said, "You are not going to tell me what to do."

I said, "Don't get in my way or any of the other men's way that are helping." When we got the pumps where they would run—without freezing weather—we started pumping the water out of the front hole.

When we got the water pumped out to where I could see the hole, I went down there. I came up and told the engineer to get me a board about a two-by-two. We don't have anything like that.

I said, "Have you got a two-by-four?"

"Yes."

"You got a Skil-saw?"

"Yes."

"Rip the two-by-four about a foot long." He brought it to me. I sharpened the two-by-two, then went to the engine room and put the part I sharpened on his grinder and turned it slow to get it round. The pumps were keeping the water pumped out and the cook had gone to her room.

I had one deckhand that seemed like he wanted to help.

He and I went down to drive the stick in the hole. I hit it very lightly and in went right on through the bottom into the river. We did not have a one-inch; now we had a two-inch hole. I was thankful the people were keeping the pumps running. I asked a man that could weld and took him down and explained what I wanted.

I said, "We are going to try and get warm. Do you have the material?"

He said, "Yes."

We went back in the deck locker to re-measure because I didn't want to have to do it over.

He said, "Give me an hour, or so."

In the galley there was a half-inch hard rubber mat by the sink. We took it to the engine room and turned the saw blade around on the Skil-saw and cut the size we needed. When the welder said, "I think I got it. Get a mattress off one of the bunks."

We took it down and threw it over the hole and we stood on the edge so the welder could build the frame for us to start with. All his welding went like clockwork except we were about to freeze. We moved the mattress, got our jack and metal and rubber mat in place. I was hoping we didn't push the bottom out. We jacked until the water quit coming in. I ask the welder did he have a piece of two-inch, or better of angle iron that would reach from the metal plate to the upper deck.

He said, "We might weld some together."

I said, "Good because if that jack gives off we will be right back where we started." He had to weld one little piece for it to be long enough.

With the water stopped and the brace in we liked one thing.

I said, "We need about a four-by-four foot concrete box around and on that plate."

We sat an electric heater where it would blow on the concrete to help it dry. We all were soaking wet from our head to our toes. I told a deckhand he could go tell the cook and captain they could come out of their room. I told the captain those pumps need to stay where they wouldn't freeze. I also told him that they weren't going anywhere and they didn't need me. Call the company and tell them I am not needed since they wouldn't be going anywhere for a few days would it be all right for me to get off. They didn't know it, but I was getting off no matter what they said.

I met the boat a year or so later and I asked how much steel did they have to put in the front hole because I knew it was rotten. It has never been fixed. I told the Captain when I got off it might hold until they got to Paducah for dry dock if they didn't run through any ice. I had tripped for these people before and they were good people to trip for.

***

The upper river freezes over in the winter. We were the first boat going into St Paul. We locked through lock ten breaking ice. As soon as we passed it would freeze over, but it wouldn't be smooth, just pieces. What we didn't know was that there was a bunch of cars way over behind some of the islands playing on the ice. When they got back to get off the ice we had messed up their route off the ice. They had to go back across the river and get winch trucks to pull them up the side of a hill.

We went into St Paul and came back out. We were coming down on lock ten when somebody shot two holes in the pilot-house windows. When we got in the lock, I went to call the office on a land phone. I told the lock man what had happened, and then he told me what they had to do to get their cars off the river. When they shot the windows out it just made a hole the size of the bullet. We put tape over the holes and it was months before they were fixed. I went back on my regular boat, which I was glad of.

Making a forty barge tow, northbound tow in New Orleans with two loads and thirty-eight empties

16. Accidents, Bridges & Teamwork

FISHERMEN

When I first started running the Atchafalaya River, Old River lock wasn't there. If the river was high when we got to the Simmesport Bridge, the boat couldn't go under the wide span, but there was a turn table bridge that the boat could go through. We would ease down to the wide span and turn our barges loose, back up and take the boat through the open span. The span that would open was wide enough to take wide boat tow through, but because of the cross current above and in the bridge it was almost impossible to make. I eased down and they turned my barges loose and I backed up to go through the open span. Just as I cleared the bridge with the boat, a hydraulic line on my steering broke.

We were floating about a half-mile behind our barges. There were two deckhands on the barges. If my rudders had been straight I could have used my engine to steer the boat. I'd seen something alongside my barges. I got my binoculars to look. There were three fishermen with boats pushing the barges to the bank. They did get the barges under a point in slack water and the deckhands got a line to the bank and tied the barges off. When we passed the barges, I told the deckhands over the PA system I would be back to get them sooner, or later.

We were a few miles below the barges before they got a new line made. I was off watch when they got the line fixed and I came back on watch facing Melville Bridge, but I made it fine.

The Atchafalaya River wasn't buoyed. There was a lake above Morgan's City that was a hit-and-miss thing. There was a buoy now and then. I went through there and it was buoyed off completely. We went up the river and came back and there weren't half-dozen buoys in the whole lake. There were some local boats that ran up through the lake. They would take cane poles and stake out a channel for them to run by and that's what we used. We tried to stay in the middle of the poles because they may be in five foot of water.

At one time the Atchafalaya River had some deep places according to the sounding machine we had; it had eighty feet on them. If you got in water over eighty feet it would go around again. There were a lot of places over a hundred feet deep. There was one place that was one hundred and forty-seven feet deep. There were a lot of fisherman that fished the Atchafalaya. This one old fisherman we would trade groceries for live catfish. Sometimes if we were northbound he would tie to the side and ride up river. He could tell me every place that was over a hundred feet deep. We did everything we could not to get in their lines or nets. It could be dangerous for your health.

We were southbound with empty barges where I was running full speed. I didn't see the fisherman in some brush. It sunk his boat and he lost all his fishing gear. To this day I don't know if we did or didn't. He said that he had four witnesses. He filed a $10,000 lawsuit against the boat. The company paid it. I asked the owner why they didn't fight it. He said that it would cost him that much to fight it, but if they report it to the Coast Guard it would go on my record. I never received anything telling me it was on record.

We passed this on to the fishermen if they couldn't be seen, they needed to come out where they could be seen when they heard a boat coming. The boats I worked on after that, we never had any trouble. We would give them a can of coffee now and then. That was about all they wanted.

WICKED BRIDGES

We were coming down the river when we got a pilot that didn't know me and I didn't know him. He went down in the deck locker where some of the men were talking. He started asking questions about my ability operating a boat. He said, "I'd like to know about the other pilot or captain I ride with."

One of the men said, "He does pretty good, but he can get real nervous around bridges."

Another said, "I get up at some of the bridges when he is on watch."

They had him thinking I shouldn't even walk on a boat, must less operate one. I noticed he would get up at every bridge that was on my watch. I just went along with it. Before I got to a bridge, I would start walking back and forth, shaking my hands. This went on from St. Louis to Baton Rouge. He had got up at ever bridge I made. I started getting in shape to make the bridge at Baton Rouge. I was just as calm as I could be. I drove the bridge and was in perfect shape when I cleared the bridge. I didn't know it but he had called the office about me being so nervous when making a bridge that they needed to get somebody to take his place. The mate went to him and told him they just made that up in the deck locker.

This pilot rode with me a few trips, when I was asked if I would transfer to a unit boat tow for the same money. That made me making more than the captain. I told the port captain I would. I was back in the black oil business. When the pilot found out I was going to transfer he told me when I got off if I needed a pilot on the unit boat tow he would like to go with me. I told him that I was going to be a relief captain, because that regular captain had been on there for years. I heard after I left the river he left the river. After he found out all the things they told him in the deck locker about me he was a good man to work with. He was a good pilot. I will admit that I watched him some for a short time. I always did this if a captain, or pilot got on the boat I didn't know. In fact, I watched all new people. I am sure a lot of people watched me.

***

We were coming down on Vicksburg Bridge and it was a little haze, you could see a mile or two. It was in the afternoon. The pilot sent a deckhand for me. We didn't have but four empty oil barges. The fog had set in where you couldn't see the first coupling, which is where the barges are put together.

I said, "If you want to, turn around and push up in the Yazoo River."

He said, "What if I turn around and just nose into the bank, and then if it clears a little I can be through the bridge in ten minutes."

I said, "That is fine. I came on watch and you couldn't see a hundred feet." This was before boats had two radars and ours wasn't doing too good.

We sat there a while and I could see the lights on top of the bridge. I called for northbound traffic below Vicksburg Bridge, Mississippi, no one answered. I moved out in the river and started floating backwards. I got within two hundred feet of the bridge and couldn't see any lights anywhere on the bridge. The ones on the hill told me I was moving. The crosscurrent above the bridge was moving me over, so I had to correct that. I had a deckhand on each side of the pilot-house watching for me.

One said, "The pier is about a hundred feet behind us and it is about a hundred feet off."

I pulled the throttles full astern. We were just about the middle of the span and just below the bridge. I could see every light on the bridge. The whole crew was on the front of the boat with life jackets on. This was not the first bridge I had backed through and it wasn't the last.

***

Usually when a pilot or captain gets on a boat, if there is something wrong, the pilot or captain getting off will give a verbal report. When I walked in the pilot-house of a twenty-five barge boat tow the captain left without saying anything. I got on at Greenville and right away I knew something was wrong.

I called the engineer and asked him to come to the pilot-house. I said, "There is something wrong with my steering."

He said, "You just got one rudder. I thought we were going in the shipyard."

One rudder, twenty-five barges and about to make Greenville Bridge—not a good start. The rudder that was still in place was on the good side to make the bridge. When I got through the bridge I started stopping so we could go to the shipyard. They sent a boat down to stand by our barges.

***

The first time I drove under the Baton Rouge Bridge with twenty-five barges, I was pilot on the boat. I was down far enough the Captain knew I wasn't going to flank.

He came up the stairs and said, "Just what do think you are doing?"

I said, "On my way to New Orleans and I knew he didn't want the controls this late in the game."

I was a little concerned, but nobody was going to know. I was in better shape when I cleared the bridge with twenty-five barges than the four piece unit tow that I had driven through the bridge. I always checked to see if there was anything in the way below the bridge before I would drive the bridge. There was a tow below the bridge waiting on me who told me it was clear all the way to capital boat store. I had just came full ahead when the boat holding up called and said a ship had just left Esso dock turning around. I got the pilot on the ship radio and told him I was driving the bridge with twenty-five loads, and where was he going to be. He said, "Out of your way." He must have told the engineer to give him all he had, because a lot of black smoke came out of his smoke stack.

When I went on a boat with a pilot or captain I didn't know, I watched them. I am sure a lot of Captains watched me. I have actually seen sweat drop off a pilot's finger and their clothes would be soaking with sweat when they got through a bad part of river or lock or bridge. I had made myself a promise that if I ever got to where I had to have something to help my nerves to do my job, it was time for me to change. There were times I just needed a break, but I never drank anything or even took an aspirin.

ACCIDENTS HAPPEN

We were southbound, when I met a boat just above Caruthersville, Missouri. He said, "Henry, the way it is down there I would wait until daylight to try and run that. It's going to be a job in the day time."

I just backed in on Blaker Boat towhead which is across the river from Caruthersville. When the Captain came up he remarked, "You had to wait for me to make this."

I said, "You just sit down and when it gets daylight I will run it."

He said, "I will run it if nobody else will."

I said, "Why don't you call the office and tell them I wouldn't run a certain place? I had put it on you, but when you do, you tell them I said I would run it when it got daylight."

It hadn't been but about three days since I saw how the channel was northbound. The river had fallen some more and the buoy boat hadn't reset the buoys. He didn't move until daylight. I walked up to the pilot-house and ask the captain did he want me to run this place since this came up on my watch and I had seen the channel about three days ago.

He said, "No, I can run it."

"Have at it then, because there is a double dog-leg

between here and where you go in on the left shore," I said and I left. (A dog-leg is where the channel makes a turn in the channel). He made one dog-leg, but not the second. I knew he could not steer the first dog-leg and make the next one. I knew he needed to back up on the first one, because it had the sharpest turn and the direction the current was running. He didn't do this and ran aground, breaking up the boat tow.

I came on watch at twelve noon. He said, "I see why you didn't want to run it at night." He was just as nice as he could be. "There is three turns on this crossing."

I said, "Recount. There are four in the middle of the river in a distance of approximate two and half miles."

We got all our barges back together about 6:00 PM.

***

We went down the river to a bend. A little bar had built up in the bend on the falling river. It was a very easy bend to steer. All the barges were out in the river, but the boat hit the bar that had built up in the bend. I jumped out of bed and got my shoes on. The barges stayed together, but it broke all the cables that were used between boat and barges and we lost a rudder on the port side. The captain said this was the worst trip he'd had in a long time. I said there was only seven hundred more miles to go! I came on watch, faced the boat up to the barges, and just started floating. Just enough power for steering.

Things were getting interesting, twenty-five miles above Memphis—bridges to make and the rudder was on the wrong side. Our flanking rudders seem to be all right. I told the Captain what my intentions were. *Did he have a better idea?* NOPE.

"I don't know if it will work, I have never seen it done, haven't ever heard of anybody doing it." I am sure it had been done, by whom and when I don't know. This was before I-40 Bridge was built. I passed the mouth of Wolf River which is at the Memphis waterfront, backing slowly. I started backing full speed. I stopped and laid the tow against the bank just above the bridge. I started backing out in the river and it was moving faster sideways than I wanted it to, so I come full ahead. I missed the right hand pier. I wouldn't have wanted to have my foot between the tow and bridge pier. It might have gotten mashed. We tied the boat tow off just above the mouth of McKeller Lake, below Memphis, and went to Greenville to the shipyard.

This tow was picked up by another boat to bring to Greenville, Mississippi. They ran aground just above Arkansas City, which is about twenty miles above Greenville, Mississippi. There were boats aground from St. Louis, Missouri to just below Baton Rouge. This tow we had was on ground five times from Cairo, Illinois, to Baton Rouge. The river had been falling fast and the buoy boats couldn't keep up. They would set a buoy, and then a big boat tow would come by and drag it off station, because the boat tow was almost as wide as the channel.

A large boat tow was up ahead of me northbound. He had loads in the middle and empties on the outside. I got to watching him dragging buoys off station when he didn't have to get close to the buoys. I called him and ask him why he was dragging those buoys off station. He told me they would have them reset before he came back down. I said what about these other boats. He said, "That's their problem."

I ran aground with two barges of asphalt. The barges were aground in the middle of the tow. We could turn the boat tow about three quarters around, but we couldn't get off. There was a boat coming down the river. I called and ask could he give me a little horsepower.

He said, "That he would like to, but he was behind schedule."

I told him thanks. I was going off watch and I just shut everything down while I talked to the pilot coming on watch. The boat tow just floated off ground while we were talking. I had, had this to happen before, but I had already tried it this time. We faced up to our barges and went on our trip.

We went to Louisville and pumped off. Coming back down the river, I heard some people talking about a boat being aground. I found out who it was. It was the boat that I had asked for a little horsepower. They were aground about half mile from where we were aground. When I passed him they had been aground about fifteen hours and the river was falling.

When I passed I said, “Captain, you have got your schedule all messed up,” and just passed right on by. Nobody offered to help them because they wouldn’t help anybody earlier. Their company paid two other companies to tie their boat tow off and help get them off ground before the river fell anymore. After that if they passed someone in trouble they would call to see if they could help.

***

I was flanking Grays point below Cape Girardea. I checked for northbound traffic below the point, or Thebes Bridge. No one answered. When I cleared the point there was a northbound boat tow below Thebes Bridge. I was on an 1800-horsepower boat and sixteen barges. Me backing full astern it would not hold the barges. I had to back under Grays Point where there wasn’t as much current. The captain came up to relieve me. I told him I would give it to him as soon as I got out of this mess.

He said, “Good, I didn’t want it anyway.”

When the boat passed I started working my way out in the current. Since the boat wouldn’t hold the barges, there was only one thing to do and that was to come full ahead. That was the closet I ever came to hitting Thebes Bridge. It was a race for the next couple miles, or so to keep the boat tow in the channel, because the tow was so out of shape when I cleared the bridge. If you got out of the channel, it was solid rock.

***

We were westbound on the canal between High Island

and Bolivar, Texas. We were pushing an empty oil boat tow unit. Our front barge had a long rake. It was called a *spoon rake* because it looked a lot like a spoon, and was a lot easier to push when loaded. On the north side of the canal, it was an island and open water to Galveston bay. On the south side there were a lot of houses and some sat right on the canal. Most of these houses sat on pilings ten or more feet above the ground. When most of these houses were built, they sat away from the canal. The channel washed a lot of the shoreline away, leaving the house right on the canal. The north wind was blowing and when I came to open water, I couldn't hold a thousand feet of empty barge up to the wind. When the boat hit the ground the barges landed on the south side of the channel. I had a feeling the bow barge hit one of those houses on pilings. I sent my mate out to see if I had hit the house.

He said, "Henry, the corner of the house is sitting on the barge." I would guess there wasn't anybody at home.

"I am going to try and ease back. Let me know what happens?" I said.

He said, "When the barge came from under the house the house dropped about a foot."

I told him to come back to the boat. I backed until I had banks on both sides, and then backed about three miles from the house. I was letting the wind hold us against the bank. I found a wide place in the canal so other boats could pass.

There was a tow about like the one I had coming up behind me. I told the captain that I was going to wait until the wind died down before I tried open water. The other tow and ours were going to load out at the same dock.

The other boat didn't get nearly as far as we had before he hit the ground. There was about fifteen hundred feet of open water on the south of the channel. When he hit bottom, his barges were blown way out of the channel and he just about had the channel closed off. We couldn't get by if the wind stopped blowing.

When the pilot came on watch, I explained what was

going on (except the house part). I told him he could do what he wanted to. He said that he wasn't going to try the way the wind was blowing even if that boat wasn't in the way.

When I came on watch at 6:00 AM the wind was still blowing. There was a boat coming up behind us with no barges. I ask him would he hold the head of my boat tow against the wind until we crossed the open water.

The captain said, "I will need to call my office."

"I wouldn't want you to unless you called your office first."

" I will call mine so he can call your office."

His office and mine had it worked out before he got to our boat. He got the head of my boat tow off the bank and here we went.

The boat that was aground in front of us had to take his cables off the boat and barge and use ropes so he could get his boat out of the channel so other boats could pass. The tide had dropped about three feet and his bow barge was out of the water. He was going to need the tide to come in before he could get his bow barge off ground.

When I passed the house the one corner had some pilings broken and the house was leaning badly. I got off watch before we got to the dock. I walked out to look at the barge. There was a little wood lying on the barge and I raked it off. That was it, except we were at the dock and loaded and gone before the other boat ever got to the dock. When we came back east, somebody had hit the house with a long rake barge and it was leveled. You could see just where the barge went. The channel had washed the banks away and the house sat right on the corner of land and open water.

I got me a recorder to record the orders that were given to me over the phone. (I had just bought the recorder and had never tried it.) I was told there was a twenty-barge boat tow on the Kentucky shore below the lower Cairo, Illinois Bridge. I asked for barge numbers, but he didn't have them yet. It would be the first tow below the bridge on the Kentucky shore. There were twenty barges made up where he told me. In fact, it was the only made up tow on that shore. We went, put out our extra rigging, and faced the boat to the barges. I played my orders back two or three times because we never used that fleet. We were almost to Memphis when the dispatcher called.

He said, "Where did you get your boat tow?"

The pilot told him we had picked it up on the Kentucky shore below the lower Cairo Bridge.

He said, "I told Henry the Illinois Shore." The pilot sent for me. I played his orders back to him. He told me that wasn't his voice.

Before I got off the boat I recorded his voice a number of times, then when I got off the boat I took my recorder by the office and played his voice and orders a number of times. He did admit it was his voice, but didn't know how he had made such a mistake. I told the dispatcher from now on he had better not be on *the weed*, when he gave me orders because they were going to be recorded.

***

We were on dry dock, or rather, a railway. They have a railway that runs out in the canal or river. They set blocks to fit the boat hull on the cradle that was on the railway, then pull the boat over the blocks and tie off.

A large winch starts pulling those blocks that were on a cradle and boat up the railway. They usually put the brake on the winch then they would block the cradle so it wouldn't go in the water.

It was about 2:00 AM and the boat moved and it woke me up. It felt like the boat moved again, then again. About every five minutes, it would move a little. I knew both tail shafts that the propeller affixed to were out of the boat. That left two eight-inch holes for water to enter the engine room if the boat got in the water. The boat had moved enough so that the ladder fell.

I went down a rope, and then I ran to the shipyard office

and told the night watchman what was happening. By the time he got somebody down there, water had ready started coming in the boat. They got us pulled back up before there was real water damage.

***

In the fifties, we were hauling crude oil out of St. Louis to Sabine Pass, Texas. The company had two boat tows on this run. One worked the northern end and one on the south end. When we met, we exchanged tows. On the south end you could go down the Atchafalaya River or you had to go through Harvey, or Algiers lock below New Orleans. This was before Port Allen, Louisiana, locks were built. We were coming down on the upper Baton Rouge Bridge. I was watching the pilot who had a lot more experience than I did, but I also knew there was a big eddy above the bridge on the Baton Rouge side. I had been in it. I was watching from below. I knew he was getting too far over to flank the bridge, I also knew he was to for down to steer the bridge. Sure enough, the head of the boat tow got in the eddy and turned us a round before you could lick your lips. I had no idea what his plans were, I was just watching. He moved back out in the river. Since we were headed against the current it was no problem to just sit there and hold the tow in place.

A deckhand came to me, said, "The pilot wants to see you."

"Tell him I will be there in a minute." I thought now what would I do.

I went to the pilot-house and the pilot was shaking so badly he could barely stand. When I saw the shape he was in, I said, "Do you want me to take the controls?" He said he did.

I drove the boat and tow up above the point which is Wilkerson point now. I turned the boat tow around headed south. I got my binoculars to see if there was any drift and which way it was floating above the bridge; this was to check the direction of the current flowing.

I had two choices—flank or drive the bridge. I asked a deckhand if everyone was up. He said they were so I said, "Tell them to put a life jacket on."

I had decided to drive the bridge. I told the engineer if I rang him a bell, give me everything those engines had. There were three things I was watching, the bridge piers, the state capitol and a big tree behind me. This would tell me how much of a slide my boat tow had and what to do. I was a little cross ways when I cleared the bridge, but in good shape. Over the years I have drove that bridge more than I flanked. I would start getting in shape when I cleared Thomas point about five miles above Wilkerson Point with a barge line boat tow. I would be just about cross ways, before I got to the point, where I would come full ahead, watching my slide.

One time I didn't hold it on the right hand pier as long as I should, but I didn't get close to the left hand pier. When I went under the bridge, my boat was just about half way between the bridge running lights and the left hand pier. If a ship was anchored above Esso docks I would flank. I never tried to flank when the river was high and water coming across Wilkerson point above the upper Baton Rouge Bridge. I tried it one time and it didn't work out very well and again it did. I didn't hit, or tear up anything.

***

I worked for one man who tried to get the captain and pilot in a mileage contest. When he told me his plans, I told him it wouldn't work. If he expected me to compete with another pilot, or captain, he could get someone to take my place. He was going to have more accidents than Carter had liver pills. (This was a saying back then if there was going to be a lot of something). I quit and in less than sixty days, his insurance was cancelled.

OFFICE WORK

I was working in the office when we needed a pilot. A man was in my office filling out an application for a pilot's job. He had on there where he had run as pilot and some references.

I said, "Let me do a little checking on this, and can you come back in an hour?"

He had worked for a number of boat towing companies and worked for the state of Texas twice. I called the people in Houston that he had worked for. They gave the okay on him, but told me that when he says, "I will be leaving in two weeks," that is what he means. I asked him if he could leave right away if things checked out. He could. I didn't have anybody to send. The port engineer and his assistant were working on a boat in the shipyard. The port captain was getting an off shore tug ready to pull a drilling rig to the Mediterranean Sea. We got in my car and went by his home, then went by my home to get something I needed to take to the boat.

We left my home and went to Monroe, Louisiana, to put him on the boat and get the other man off. We had talked all the way to the Monroe and I just picked up a little now and then about his past and him working for the state. I got back home about 6 AM. His name just kept ringing a bell, but I couldn't place it.

I had just finished reading about a murder case where a woman hired a man to kill her husband. About ten minutes before I got home, it came to me. His name was in this book. I went in the house, got the book and started checking some dates he gave me when he worked for the state and they matched up with the date he had told me. I told my wife that the man I just took to Monroe was in the book. He was hired to kill her husband for ten thousand dollars, then backed out. When I met the boat in Port Arthur, Texas, I took him off to one side.

I said, "It makes no difference one way or other, but I am fixing to ask you a question. Was you hired to kill that woman's husband?"

He said yes. He was paid ten thousand dollars and then backed out. He continued, "I spent the money and didn't do the job. Somebody told the police I had accepted money to murder someone."

I think he told me he got five years. He was a good pilot, everybody liked him and he could do wonders with a boat. He did tell me since he was hired to kill the man, he hasn't drank a drop of alcohol. Ironically, another company offered him more money and he gave me a two weeks' notice.

***

While I worked in the office, I got to know a lot of people that were in some way connected to boats. A number of these people were with oil companies that let oil movement contracts.

I'd been gone from the company about three years. I was in a bank in Houston when I met up with one of these men. He and I got to talking and he told me what he was looking for. I thought about it for myself and my brother, but we had already been in the boat business and I didn't want any more. I told him about a man that had one boat and two barges that seemed to be just what he was looking for. I called the boat owner and ask him would he be interested in job hauling both ways from Houston to Corpus. If he was, call so-and-so at the number I gave him.

The boat owner got a two-year contract with an option of a year at a time after the two years were up. I decided I wanted to make a couple trips to Corpus. I called him to see if he needed anybody to make a couple trips or even one trip. He wouldn't even talk to me.

I had known this man a long time and it came as a shock that he wouldn't even talk to me. His son and I decked together. I called his wife and to see if I did something to cause him not to talk to me. She said she didn't know. For some reason I let this upset me. Two, or three years later I had to go see a man at a shipyard in Houston. We were having lunch when I brought this man's name up.

He said, "I won't work on any of his equipment."

When he got that contract and started making the money he was making, he changed. He brought his boat into my yard twice and I haven't seen him after the second time. He wanted me to stop what we were working on to dry dock his boat. I had a boat on my dock and he wanted me to take the boat of dock and put his on. I told him to go somewhere else. It seems the money went to his head.

HENRY HELPS

I had been tripping for a few months and decided I was going to take off a while. I was lining out what me and my family were going to do the next sixty days. A company called, wanted me to go from Baton Rouge to Corpus Christi and back to Baton Rouge. I told them I was going to take sixty days off.

He told me what he would pay me, which was about twenty-five percent above the going rate for the river. I left to go to Baton Rouge, when I got off the plane there was a message for me to call the office. Another company had called my house wanting me. My wife told them where I had gone and who for. The second company called the first and wanted to borrow me.

"I have hired him to go to Corpus. If you will let me have Henry, I can cover you on the Corpus trip." The first company told the second company what the pay was. I can handle that for the days they needed me. I flew from Baton Rouge to Charleston, West Virginia, where I got on a boat for Cairo, Illinois. They had changed plans and I got off at Point Pleasant, West Virginia because the boat was going into Pittsburgh. I called the company to ask if they have me a plane ticket to somewhere between Pittsburgh to Baton Rouge and they told me to call the company they borrowed me from. I called them and I would get on the boat I was supposed to have, because they had to go into the shipyard. I had not been to bed since I left home. I had been gone over three days. I did get a little sleep on the planes and the cab from Point Pleasant, West Virginia, to Pittsburgh Airport.

My wife asked me how I could go so long without any sleep. I was a person that did not need much sleep. Usually after lunch, I would go to bed about 1 PM. By two-thirty or three, I was up. When I got off watch at midnight, I would go to bed about 1 AM and would get up by 4 AM. When I stood the midnight to 6 AM watch, I would be wide awake until about 2 AM. From 2 to 4 AM it was rough on me to stay awake. I never sat down. I get off watch at 6 AM. I would be in bed by 6:30. By 8:30 I would be up. When I got off watch at 6 PM, I couldn't go to sleep until about 10 PM; that would give me about an hour and half before I came on watch. I have walked a lot miles in the pilot-house to stay awake. I did a lot of walking when on and off the boat anyway. When we went into a dock where I could, I would walk four or five miles.

***

I and a couple other Captains had helped this man make pilot. Before they got my help, they had to have worked in the engine room, helped the cook in the galley, or anything else. I wanted him to know that none of it was easy before he started laying the blame on someone else. This man I had just turned loose to stand watch.

I said, "You are on your own, but if I see you are fixing to mess up, I will tell you. When you get to island so-and-so, don't try to run behind it."

I went down stairs and I looked out. I could see willow bushes on both sides. I broke and run to the pilot-house and pushed him out of the way to put both engines full astern. I didn't have time to try and explain why. It made him mad and I was already mad, but we hit ground before the tow was stopped.

I said, "I told you not to run behind this island and you

did it anyway. That just about does it for me."

He said, "I looked at your marks and they showed we had plenty of water."

"Those marks are for a rising river." Then, I showed him the marks on falling river. "You don't ever want to use someone else's marks—your hundred yards maybe different than mine. If the company wants to put you on another boat that is fine, but you can't ride with me."

This was back when a Captain was *the Captain*; I put him off at Hickman, Kentucky. He was put on another boat, but he didn't last long. He had got mile happy. I had told him the office didn't expect him to make the miles I did until he learned where to run. Back then there were a lot of places you could run that you can't today with the same river stage.

***

Once, I was tied off in a radio dead zone and the office was trying to contact me. There was a boat about twenty miles away and he was in the operator's range. The office message had to be relayed to me through him. A few of the first boats I worked on didn't have radios except for a receiver, but did not allow transmitting. When we reached a land phone, we'd call home. It cost one dollar and seventy-five cents for three minutes for a hundred mile call at a pay phone.

The Captain is in charge of the boat and crew. As Captain, my main concern was the safety of my crew. If you take care of them, they'll take care of you. Every Captain had a different way of doing things. I've worked with Captains who could care less about the crew's safety, or their problems. Crew members have problems on and off the boat. I tried to be a help to them when I could and a person they could come to about their problems. They were away from home and needed to talk with someone. You were their Captain, counselor, mother, father, and sometimes, minister.

You were given orders from the office and carried them

out to best of your ability. At times they were willing to put more on you, placing your boat and crew at risk. I've been given orders to pick up barges that I have, at times, refused to take. If the engineer needed help from a crew member, the Captain made sure the engineer received help. I've had a few engineers who would try to take advantage of this assistance.

I can recall one engineer who came to me for help. I left watch and walked down the outside of the boat to check things out. The engineer was sitting, drinking coffee, and the two men sent to help were doing all the work. I walked in the engine room. When he saw me, he jumped right in with the men. At first sight, I noticed his hands weren't even dirty. On the other hand, the helpers were covered in grease. He and I had a good understanding after this. I've called on an engineer to help my men if they needed help, so it worked both ways.

One time, all the deckhands were putting some barges together after we hit ground. I had no one to catch me a line off the boat to the barges. I called the cook and asked would she go to the forward deck and get a line to a deckhand. She could throw and tie a line off a lot better than most deckhands.

A good captain tries to keep expenses down while making sure his people have the equipment needed to do their jobs. You need a good working relationship with office personal. If you do have contact with your company customers, have a good relationship with them as well. (I've seen an ill-mannered captain cause the company to lose the renewal of a good contract.) The customer may be wrong, but let the company tell the customer he or she is wrong. If a customer asked for my opinion I'd say, "This is my opinion and my opinion only," or, "I really don't have an opinion," or, "You need to talk to my office."

The Captain has another important role—making sure the cook is preparing good food that the crew will eat. If a cook asks me what I prefer, I'd tell them to, "Watch and fix what the crew will eat. I'll eat anything that doesn't eat me first."

There was one exception. If a cook knew a crew member had a birthday they'd usually bake a birthday cake. I had about six birthdays a year. I'd tell the cook, "Well, I will be a year older tomorrow."

"What kind of cake do you want?"

"German Chocolate," I responded without hesitation.

I went on another company boat and I'd forgotten this was the cook that made me a cake a couple months before.

"Well, tomorrow I will be a year older."

"German Chocolate."

Later, I came down to eat. She said, "Henry, how many birthdays do you have a year?"

I said, "About six."

The Captain stands two watches a day out of twenty-four hours. The first is from 6 AM 'til twelve noon and 6 PM 'til midnight. The pilot stands the other two watches getting the boat and barge up and down the river, the captain has logs and other paperwork he needs to be doing. There are times when a Captain is off watch and he may have to get up to take care of some issue. He has a mate that is in charge of making boat tow. If the mate discovers bad equipment, finds that someone isn't doing their job, or realizes a crew member is a troublemaker—on down the line—he reports this to the Captain. The Captain takes necessary steps to solve the problem.

17. Family

For years when I left home my wife could tell you who I working for, but after a while, it became impossible to keep up. The owner of a company called me the loan-out pilot. I made better money this way. There was one company that paid me five days a month whether or not I worked. When I had time or they needed me, I would go work for them. If I worked thirty days, I got five days' pay on the first of the month payday. Sometimes I would owe them and sometimes they would owe me. My insurance came out of this five days' pay.

Working on a boat is hard on family life. It makes no difference if you were a deckhand, cook, engineer, pilot, or captain. These people are gone from home at least fifty-percent of the time. The wife raised the children with firm discipline and took care of anything that came up around the home. The wife depended on other family members, or if no family members were around, she depended on friends and church members. She had to make decisions, all decisions—alone. And riverboat husbands had to accept them right or wrong.

Back when I started working on the boats, you didn't just pick up a phone and call home, and your wife just couldn't pick up a phone and call you. We had to go through a marine operator and we always had trouble getting calls to go through. Everybody on the marine operators channel could hear both sides of the conversation. As years went by, things did get better, but even then a lot of times the boat would be in a dead zone.

My family would ride with me sometimes. I had told them all when they saw me stand up, don't be asking me any questions. I got my mind on operating the boat. When they rode, it may be one or all. I had three children and my wife. The boys wanted to work on the boats. I told them they could choose to do whatever they wanted to, but I didn't want them to be a lawyer. This is because you would have to defend a person even if they were guilty. I had wanted to be a lawyer in my early years. I sat in a lot of courtrooms while in the service and learned the ins-and-outs of being a lawyer. I realized it wasn't for me. I could not defend somebody I knew was guilty.

All in all, working on boats you will be away from your family over half your life.

The first time my wife rode with me, she wasn't sure about living on a boat. She would hear something and say, "What was that?" She got used to it after a while.

Sometimes, my family would get on at Greenville and go north or south, then get off at Greenville when we came back through. Sometimes one of the boys would go back with me and ride until I got off. Greenville was the best place for them to get on and off. Vicksburg was closer to my home, but I had a friend in Greenville where my wife could leave the car.

***

I had the owner's son decking on the boat. One day I told him that if he didn't start to carry his load I was sending him home.

He said, "You can't fire me, because my daddy owns the company."

I called the port captain and told him what I was going to do. He said, "Henry, I wouldn't do that," so I called the boy's father. I said, "I am sending your son home," and explained why.

He said, "I will get somebody to take his place."

I got off in a couple days and the boy's mother called me twice. Boy, was she mad.

"Don't you know his daddy owns the company?"

I said, "I sure do, and your son needs to carry his load just like everybody else."

A day, or two later she called again. When my wife told me who it was I started to tell my wife I didn't want to talk to her, but I did. She said, "Henry, after my husband explained the things to me, I wanted to call and tell you I am sorry I called you about my son. My husband told me out of six Captains, you were the only one that would make him do his work and I want him to do his work and do it right."

I thanked her for the call and I would see he did his work or he would be back home.

Later, I needed a deckhand and the owner asked could his son come back. I said that he would have to carry his load or I would send him home again.

The owner said, "I don't think you will have any problem, but if you do, put him off."

The boy didn't tell me, but he told someone on the boat, "Getting fired was nothing until I got home. You should have heard the way my daddy talked to me. I was ready to get back on the boat before daddy had finished."

He made a real good deckhand. He was always ready to do what he was told and a lot of things he seen needed to be done without being told.

I talked to him later and he told me how glad he was that I had put him off. He said he had grown up more in twenty-four hours that he thought was possible.

He called me a few times after I had changed companies to see how I was doing. On a boat everybody has a job and if one doesn't do his, that means somebody else has to pick what he's supposed to be doing; it makes double work for the others. After he finished school he came and worked for me with another company.

***

There was a man that had been running as mate for a few years with different companies. When I changed jobs and I got an opening, I would hire him. He knew how I operated and I knew how he operated. I had noticed for a day or so he didn't have much to say. I thought he had something on his mind he didn't care to talk about. I knew he was having trouble with his son-in-laws.

I had some book work I needed to do so I got him up there to steer the boat for me. I was doing my paperwork in the pilot-house and now and then I would say something to him. He never said a word. When I finished, I asked him to get one of the deckhand to do something. In about two minutes, he came back to the pilot-house.

He had a steel rod and said, "Henry, I am going to kill you." I had a deckhand over six feet tall and big. He had noticed this mate had been acting a little funny. He saw the mate go get the rod and start to the pilot-house and he followed him. I had no way to defend myself from where I was in my chair to where he was with the rod. This big deckhand grabbed the rod and took it away from him. The mate sat down in the floor and cried like a baby. He acted like he didn't know anyone.

I called his wife and explained what had happened and she asked could she come and get him. It was about a three hours' drive to the place where we could put him off and she could get to him. He just cracked up. We got him off the boat, he didn't know any of his family. There was enough family to keep an eye on him twenty four hours a day. The doctors wanted to put him in a mental hospital where he could be watched around the clock. The wife chose to take him home.

Now and then I would call. Always the same. He was going to the doctor in Memphis. This had been going on over a year. Wherever she took him, she always had one of the men that were kin to go with them.

Well over a year from the beginning of day one, they were going to the doctor when he said, "Where are we going?"

He knew both of them, where he was and everything. He was never able to return to work. He kind went off and on until he died.

***

The company was having a Captain's and Chief Engineer's meeting in Memphis and the spouses were invited. All the captains wanted to know who was bringing their wife. Some knew that I would rent a car and drive home sometimes. They ask me was I going to drive or fly. At that time out of Tyler, Texas, there was a little plane that had three seats across the back of the plane. When asked was I going to fly, I would say, "If I knew I could get the backseats on the little plane out of Tyler, I would fly."

This was my answer to anybody that asked me, "Why the back seat?"

"Well, my wife is so large it takes two seats for her."

The office called to see about making the reservation, I told them to let me think about, and I told her the same thing. I said go ahead and make the reservations and I would take my chances. None of these people had ever met my wife. She was about five-feet and seven inches tall and weighed about one hundred and twenty pounds.

The office crew plane was due in Memphis about the same time as ours, but at a different baggage claim. I told my wife to wait while I went to see if the office crew had made it. They had, so I went and got my wife and our baggage and went where they were. I introduced my wife to one of the men.

He said, "Mrs. Elliott, Henry is a pretty good fellow, but is also the biggest liar in Texas." I went to another man and introduced her.

He said, "Mrs. Elliott, do you know what Henry has been saying about you?

She said, "No telling."

One of the women came over to me and said, "Your wife should kill you. We all were looking for your wife to be large."

We all went to the motel. After we got checked in and got our rooms, my wife and I went downstairs where we met another Captain. I introduced them. He looked at her, and then looked at me. He didn't know what to say. Finally, he said, "Pleased to meet you."

He went on to the bar, my wife and I went somewhere else. This Captain told another person that I had the strongest nerves of anybody he had ever ridden a boat with. I also had the most gall of anybody he had ever seen. They asked why and he said bringing that woman up and introducing her as my wife. His wife is a great big woman.

Eventually, though, they were convinced she was my wife.

HEALTH SCARE

My port captain called to see if I could go to Vermillion locks and get on a boat to help some people out. The Captain had died in Baton Rouge and the pilot was the only pilot on there. The only way for me to get to Vermillion locks was for my wife to take me and she needs get somebody to go with her. He called the company and they told my port captain they would pay her and the person to go with her and all expenses. It's a long ways from where I lived to Vermillion locks. When I got to Vermillion lock, I told my wife for her and her mother to get a motel room. I had reminded my port captain that I was to catch my boat in about two days.

He said, "I can cover you there."

The pilot and I were both give out, but said for him to get a few hours' sleep then I would wake him. I found out how the captain was acting before he died. They said that he had been talking about his chest and left arm hurting. When we left Texas City, I would walk around feeling of my arm and chest. I would know people were watching, but I would try to act like I was hiding it. By the time we got to the Mississippi River, everybody's arm and chest was hurting. When we got to Greenville where we were pumping off, everybody that wasn't getting off to go home, wanted to go get a checkup. It was a good thing, because one was on the verge of having a heart attack. They kept him in the hospital until they got him in shape to go home. He didn't know anything was wrong with him.

18. "Old" New Boats

There were three boats the U.S. Marshall was about to put on the block for sale. This company wanted to buy them before the Marshalls got them. The company owner called me and he said, "I have had those three boats surveyed. There is an engineer on each boat. I would like for you to go find out what you can about what is wrong with the boats. They are tied up at Wood River, Illinois."

I made it to St. Louis, got a motel, and changed into old work clothes and I had bag with some things in it. I rented a car and I put it in a parking lot about a mile from the boats. I went down the road with my bag to these boats.

The three engineers were sitting outside.

I said, "Are you all doing any hiring?"

"No, these boats are for sale, you want to buy them?" the man asked.

I said, "Not hardly."

They offered me coffee and we talked. I told them I'd worked on a tug in the canal, I didn't say when. They gave me tour of all the boats. I said, "Working on a boat this big and all this room would be living like a king."

On those tours, I found out more than I expected. I went back up the road with enough information; no one would have bought them if they knew what I knew. I went back to the motel where I called the man that hired me.

I said, "You may want to get your secretary to write this

down." He put her on the line and I read everything I had. "Tell your boss I will call him back after he goes over this to see if he has any questions."

I stayed around the motel until it was almost time for me to go to the airport. I called the man to see if he had any questions about what I had given his secretary. He wanted to know how I got all this information. I told him it all came from the three engineers. I said I told them I had been working in the canal on tugs. This was no lie, because I *had* worked on a tug in the canal. I just didn't tell them when.

They gave me a tour of all three boats. I said, "Boy, this must be the life on those bigger boats." One said that when he went to work on this boat it was in good shape, but they wouldn't spend the money to keep it up. Another one said that it would take more to fix them up, than what they would sell for.

He said, "Henry, you should see the reports the surveyor gave me. He reported a few things wrong, but nothing like you told me."

I said, "Everything I gave you is from people that have been working on the boats. I had seen a number of things wrong they never mentioned. This is my opinion from the way the engineer talked. The owner was taking all the income, putting it away and letting the boats run down. One of the engineers said that the owner owed over three hundred thousand dollars, for shipyard repairs that had to be done, fuel, groceries and other supplies for all the boats."

Months later, I found out a good friend of mine had bought one of the boats. I saw him at the shipyard and the boat he had bought was on dry dock. I said, "Isn't that one of three boats that was for sale at Wood River a few months ago." (I knew it was; it had a new name and was repainted).

My friend said, "Yes, and the biggest piece of junk I ever bought. I had a survey on this boat before I bought it. It wasn't bad, so I purchased it. I never got one trip out of it before things started happening. I have had both main engines and generator completely overhauled. One of the gears had to be overhauled. It looked like a welding rod had touched some of the gears. Had to do a lot of rewiring and get all new electronics in the pilot-house."

I'd heard enough, but I knew he put several hundred thousand dollars in the boat which wasn't worth near what he had in the boat. I never did tell him I'd found out all about the boats for another party. He had a good boat now, but it was old and with no major breakdowns, it would take years to get his money back, if he ever did. What fooled a lot of people was how clean and painted up they were. You could have eaten off the engine room floor.

This took me back to my first year, or so on the boats. The company was going to sell one of their boats. There were holes rusted in the handrail and few other places. They got us masking tape to tape the handrails and other places. We put so much paint on the tape until you couldn't see the tape. The night before the people came to look at the boat, it came a flood of rain and a lot of this tape came off. The people came on the boat and they were there about a minute and left. The company still had the boat when I left the company—rusty hand rails and all.

Retractable pilot-house, lowers to go under low bridges

19. Riverboat Cooks

I went on this boat and the cook couldn't boil water without burning it; she couldn't cook a thing. I asked the Captain when we were going to get a cook, but he was satisfied with her cooking. Every time they passed Memphis or Greenville, people were quitting because of the food. She once cooked a cake you couldn't cut with a regular table knife. It sat on the table about a week and I threw it over the side. The cook came down the next morning said, "Oh boy, somebody ate my cake. I will have to make another." And she did. I don't know what she put in her cakes to make them so hard.

***

I was Captain on another boat and we hired a cook in Memphis. I didn't eat breakfast. The mate asked, "Henry, did you go down and eat some of those biscuits this morning?"

"No," I answered.

The next morning it was the same thing. The third morning I decided to go try the biscuits out. I asked the cook to give me a couple eggs over easy and she put some bread in the toaster. I said, "I want biscuits."

"I can't cook biscuits and as long as I am on this boat there won't be any."

I said, "We have a bunch of biscuit eaters on here."

"They will just have to eat some other kind I bread," she said.

"I will be back in a few minutes," I said, as I left to relieve the pilot then turned it over to the mate. This mate was a good pilot in fact he had been a pilot, but his nerves wouldn't take it. Afterward, I went back to the galley and told the cook she and I needed to have a talk.

"About what?" she asked,

I said, "Biscuits."

She said, "I thought that was settled."

I said, "No. It's like I told you. We have a bunch of biscuit eaters on here and they are going to have biscuits."

She said, "I will order a bunch of canned biscuits, then."

"They want homemade biscuits and that is what they are going to get," I said. "Just be quiet and listen. We are going to be in Memphis in a couple days. Have your bags packed, because you will be getting off."

"You can't fire me because the boat store hired me."

"You got that wrong. When I want a crewmember, I call the boat store and tell them what I want, and they will get me the person I need. It just so happens they sent me a body that can't cook biscuits."

She started crying and I got up and went to the pilot-house. I told the mate what had happened.

The mate passed through the galley and she asked, "Do you think I can talk to the Captain?"

"Anybody can talk to that man as long as they use a little sense." She had never been to the pilot-house, so the mate showed her the way. "If he is busy, just ask when would it be a good time to talk to him."

That she did. I said, "Right now is as good as any. Just move over here so you won't be talking to the back of my head and I won't be talking to the front glass."

She asked, "Are you firing me because I can't cook biscuits?"

I answered, "No, because you won't try. Let's us have an understanding, it's not what I want to eat, but what my crew wants to eat."

"Can I keep my job if I learn how to cook biscuits and anything else the crew wants?"

I said, "Have the crew wake me about 4 AM. I will get up and show you how to make biscuits." I did this two mornings. The third morning I was going to let her cook and I would watch. When the biscuits came out of the oven, they were about the size of a silver dollar. I knew she had put just the right stuff in the mixing bowl. She was just sick.

I said, "We will try them again in the morning."

The next morning, I went down and got a new can of baking powder and she mixed the biscuit dough up. The biscuits turned out great. It came to me what happened; I told the mate what I did to my mother-in-law one time. I called the mate to the pilot-house, told him that was a dirty thing he pulled on the cook and me.

"What did I do?"

"You poured the baking powder out and filled the baking powder can with flour."

He said, "Henry, I think you told me how to do that."

We had biscuits three times a day until she learned how to cook cornbread. She turned out to be a great cook and baker. Soon, she could make the best yeast rolls you ever laid your lips to. I asked her how she raised five kids and never learned to cook.

"My mother-in-law lived with us. She took care of the kids and house," she said.

I told her if she needed to look for a job cooking, she could use my name. She said, "If you needed a cook, call me." She did cook for me again.

***

We had this one cook that you knew to never mention her grandchildren. If you did that was the last word you would get in. I learned in a hurry. We would be sitting around the table and when I would ask how her grandchildren were, they would get up and leave to let the others to listen. We knew just about every time a diaper had been changed. The crew learned if I started to ask her anything, no one would be around the table before I got the question out.

***

I received a call from a woman in Mississippi. She informed me that she was in need of a cooking job and a certain person had referred her to me.

I asked, "Can you boil water without burning it?"

She said if she couldn't she didn't need a job and the state should be taking care of her.

I said, "You will have to start as a maid, then when the cook gets off you will be the cook." I told her when to be in Memphis.

That woman's name liked to have blown my mind. I couldn't help but laugh when she told me. I explained her job to her and if she had any questions to ask the cook or me. I thought if she was as good cook as she was as a maid she should work out. The cook got off and this woman took the cook's place. She was a better cook than our regular cook. She was easy to get along with and the crew loved her. When the main cook came back and I didn't know the boys had been telling her what a good cook this other woman was and how easy she was to get along with. We were northbound, and about two hours before we got lock forty-one at Louisville, she said that she was quitting.

I said, "That's not much of a notice." And she told me what had been going on. I said, "I can put a stop to that."

"Never mind. I was getting ready to quit anyway," she responded.

I told her again that I would put a stop to them talking about the other cook. She said that it was time for her to go.

We had a deckhand that was a good cook. I ask him would he cook until we got us a cook and he agreed. I called the cook from Mississippi (the one with the funny name) and asked her when she could get on the boat. I told her that I could get her a plane ticket to Cincinnati if she could leave right away.

"I'm not going to get on a plane," she spouted.

I said, "Get you a bus ticket to Cattlesburg, Kentucky. If you get there before we do, get you a motel room, and if we have passed, you can get a cab on up the river." She agreed so I gave her a number to call when she arrived. She got on and I told her she was the regular cook now if the regular Captain didn't have any objections. Now we had to get a maid that could cook.

She said, "I know a woman who has been working at a motel cleaning rooms and cooking."

I asked, "Can you write her a letter and see if she wants a job on the boat?"

I called the regular Captain at home and told him what had gone on and ask was it all right to hire a woman that the cook knew. He said it was fine with him. The regular Captain and maid got on and I got off. When I came back, everything was running smoothly. Usually, when I came back everybody was in a bad mood. The regular Captain had to get off so the pilot got on and we went on north.

We were going into the boat owner's dock to pump off. It was after lunch, the cook had lain down and the maid had gone up on the dock to make a phone call. She came back and woke the cook up. The owner and his wife were going to be there for supper.

"You had better get up so we can be ready."

The cook told the maid, they were human just like us. "He may own this boat and this dock, but they put their drawers on just like we do—one leg at a time."

Later, the owner and his wife, the maid, the cook, and myself, were talking. The cook spoke with regular Mississippi country talk. She said, "Mr. and Mrs. *So-and-So,* I have a question I would like to ask you all."

"What is it?"

"Do you all put your drawers on like us country folks do, one leg at a time?"

I liked to have fell off my stool, but the owner said, "We sure do. If anybody tells you different, they are wrong. Unless they have practice jumping up and getting both legs in at one time. If they do that, they aren't as old as we are."

That cook stayed for years after I had left.

***

Myself, my cook, and couple others were getting off in Wood River. A boat had run aground and the boat store boat couldn't get to us. After about four hours, we changed crews. We were at the boat store waiting on our ride to the airport and the cook's suitcase was right next to mine. I went to get mine and noticed blood coming out of her suitcase. I told her next time she took meat off the boat to be sure and wrap it up good, because her suitcase was bleeding. She picked it up and I thought she went to the bathroom. She had called a cab, which we didn't know until someone told us. I never saw or heard from her again.

***

I went on a boat and I didn't know a single person. I went and sat down to eat breakfast and the cook was about as big around as she was tall.

She asked, "What will you have for breakfast?"

I asked for a couple hard fried eggs, couple pieces burnt toast and a cup of cold coffee so I would feel at home. The same morning, she cooked two hard fried eggs, two pieces toast, and poured up a cup of coffee. The next morning she served me what she cooked the morning before.

She said, "I sure want you to feel at home, now eat that, you little fat *so-n-so*." Then she fixed my breakfast.

***

I was running Captain; I had two of my East Texas cousins working on the boat with me. We were on our way from Houston to Corpus Christi on the Intracoastal Canal. The cook had a toothache that was getting worse and there was no place he could get it pulled. My cousins told him they would pull it. He refused until he began hurting so badly and he asked for their help.

They laid him on the dining table and found a pair of pliers. The cook said, "I know I'll raise Cain, but hold me and get that tooth out." Sure enough, he did struggle, but they got the tooth. The cook said, "You pulled the wrong tooth."

One cousin said to the other, "Catch him and we will get the right one." But the cook wasn't going for that.

20. Accidents Happen

We were coming down the river and we were to pick up a barge at New Madrid, Missouri. Barges have a letter, or letters, then a number, like CC 200. The pilot called and told the harbor service we were to pick up a certain barge. I was on watch when we got there. When the harbor boat was bringing the barge out, I checked the number, but not the letters. We were below Vicksburg, Mississippi, when the office called.

"Do you have *so & so* barge?" I told them, "Yes. I was told they had one in their fleet at New Madrid." They told me to check the letters. I sent the mate out to get the letters and I had picked up the wrong barge because the mate didn't look at the letters. This was something that happened pretty often, but it was the first time for me.

The barge we had was going to New Orleans, which was fine, since that was our destination. It ended up costing the company a pretty penny. We had boat towed this barge for over four hundred miles for nothing, plus on to New Orleans for nothing. Now, the company would have to pay another boat towing company to pick up the barge we were to pick up. I told the company I messed up. They wanted to know why the mate hadn't checked to make sure it was the right barge (that was his job). It was my fault, even if he was supposed to check, so I said, "Drop it here and now." It was never mentioned again.

I have made my share of mistakes over the years, but I was always up front and honest about them. I have taken the blame for mistakes I didn't think I made, unless there was a question mark there. If somebody tried to blame me for something where there was a question mark, I would say *prove it.*

***

We were pumping liquid sulfur off in Cincinnati when a hose busted. The sulfur was over 260 F°. The dock foreman and I were on the barge talking when the hose busted. He had his back to the hose and I was facing it. We were far enough away that it was just a spray, but it hit me in the face and blinded me. The company sent their plane up there after me, to fly me home. I was going to the eye doctor every day. He would put something in my eyes and then put something over my face. This went on about two weeks before my vision came back in the left eye. It took about ten days before the vision came back in my right eye. The only time they hurt was if I walked from a bright to dark place. It was about three months before I could return to work. I had to have reading glasses at forty-seven. I didn't need glasses to see distance until I was well into my seventies.

***

Once, I was coming out of the Ohio River headed up the Upper Mississippi. I called for southbound traffic coming out of the upper river. No one answered so I got in shape to go around Cairo point. Whoa! Here came a whole river full of barges out of the upper Mississippi River. I threw my rudders hard down to the port and headed down the Mississippi just to stay out of the barges' way. The Captain had under or over flanked, his barges hitting a sandbar. His boat hit the bank, knocking the rudders off. Sixteen or so barges were on the loose. When the harbor tugs got all the barges rounded up, I got them to help me turn around.

The pilot had fallen and hurt himself. He had to go to the hospital below Natchez, Mississippi. I called the office and told them I needed a pilot. They flew one in and landed on a sandbar. Our johnboat went after him. When I saw who it was I called the office, I told them that man was no pilot.

"Well, he has got licenses," the office person said.

I said, "I can't help what kind of licenses he's got, but he is no pilot. I rode the boat with him for one watch."

I had given him the controls. Within fifteen minutes I had to take the control back. He could not steer the boat tow. I told him he would be getting off at Vicksburg, Mississippi. I stood watch on to Greenville, where I got a pilot. I have often wondered how he got his license in the first place. He got so many jobs, until he finely gave up. I was told he lost his licenses because of accidents. I do not know for sure. This is when a captain has to do things he doesn't like to do. I never liked to call the office about another pilot or anybody. If it was a fellow pilot, I usually let him hear what I had to say to the office; I did not go behind his back.

***

I was on a boat that was underpowered for the boat tow we had. It wouldn't push Grays Point, below Cape Girardeau, Missouri, on the upper river. I just kept moving over closer to the point. When I stuck the nose of my tow out in the current, I did keep it from turning around, but we went backwards down the river. A lite boat was coming up the river that helped me around the point.

***

We were coming out of St. Louis with all the barges we needed. The dispatcher called and told me to pick a barge up at Cape Girardeau. I told him that I was not going to try and make Thebes Bridge with a barge hanging on the side. He put the big boss man on the line. I told him the same thing. H said okay, so I thought it was settled. About 4:30, the dispatcher called back. The pilot sent a deckhand after me.

"This is Henry."

"Henry, we have got to get that barge at Cape Girardeau."

I said, "I told you this morning I wasn't going to try Thebes Bridge with a barge hanging on the side when we have more than we need already."

He said, "We have got to get that barge, no matter."

I was on watch when we got to Cape Girardeau. I called the harbor boat and told him that I needed to take a barge out of my boat tow and put one in. The dispatcher was getting what he wanted and I was doing what I told him I wouldn't do. The next morning, I didn't need a telephone to hear the dispatcher.

"You said we had to get that barge so we both got what we wanted. We picked up the barge you wanted us to, and I didn't have one on the side.

The boat that picked up the barge I dropped, put it on the side and had a disaster at Thebes Bridge.

When the companies started building larger boats with more horsepower and much larger boat tows, the river wasn't ready yet. The river was not stabilized enough with rock dikes. The big boat tows ran aground and blocked the channel so often, dragging buoys off station. This might have put a rush on putting the dikes in.

One year, the river got low and a sandbar built up above the Greenville Bridge. You had to flank to where you would re-flank onto the Arkansas shore. Then you go under a point on the Arkansas shore and run the span of the bridge until they got a dredge in there. I never had to do it but one time because of the sandbar. I have flanked under the point when a boat would be stalled-out in the bridge so he wouldn't have to drop back. It was a double flank. There have been a number of boats stalled-out in Greenville Bridge when they would get too far one way or another and hit a bridge. There have been a number of boats sunk at the Greenville Bridge because they stalled-out and a number of people lost their lives.

***

We were going up river under the Memphis Railroad where you would cross the river and run up the Arkansas side. While up river, it had changed where we went down between two islands, and I hadn't read my channel report. By the time I saw the channel had been moved, it was too late. I had empty barges; the boat hit the bottom solid and there went my barges. They were floating in shallow water and I couldn't get them. They floated down through the bridges and I caught them below. This was a long time before I-40 Bridge was built. There was a barge line boat tow coming down behind me. He ran the way the channel was marked. He ran aground, too, and barges went everywhere.

I would say that in my years of running the Mississippi River, at some point and time, most of the channel has been on both sides of the river (not at once) between Natchez, Mississippi, and Cairo, Illinois.

At Montgomery Bend, I stayed at my flank too long. I tried to out run the sandbar on the port side to Victoria Bend. I knew I was going too fast try to slow enough to flank Victoria Bend. If I had tried to stop, it would have been a disaster. It could be a disaster on any decision I made. I called the engineer and asked if the engines had any more RPMs left. He gave me what I needed. That's when you use nerves you didn't know you had and make the right judgment call.

OFFICE WORK

Once, I was working in the office when I passed the accounting department. I heard one lady complaining about the boat crews, their wives, and paychecks. A wife had called in that she hadn't received her husband's paycheck. I stopped when I passed the door to listen. This lady in the accounting department got real ugly with the man's wife.

"Your husband's d--- check was mailed out a week ago," she barked and then hung up.

I went on to my office and the crew member's wife called me. I told her I was passing the payroll department when they were talking. I said, "Until I get this check thing straightened out, how much money do you need?"

She said, "I can make it to the next payday if it is on time."

I told her I would have a check in her hand with in twenty-four hours, if that was okay. She said that will be fine.

I called the woman in charge of payroll and told her to find out when this employee's check had been made out and mailed. She checked; it had never been made out.

I said, "I want a check in my hand as soon as it is signed. I want all the payroll employee's to come to my office." When they got there I said, "I know this is a mistake somebody made and I know everybody makes mistakes, but from now on, I want you all to be more understanding. Think what would happen if you never got your check and you had bills waiting to pay. Here's something else you might keep in mind; the boat crew doesn't have a job because of you. You have a job because of them. They are the ones that bring the bacon home. Just think on those two things. That's all."

The woman in charge of payroll said, "I will have you a check in about twenty minutes." When she brought me the check, she said, "You said something that has made us all stop and think how right you are. We have been talking about it ever since we got back to the office."

When I got the employee's check in my hand I called the wife. I knew she worked four or five blocks from the office. I offered to bring the check to her.

She said, "If you will leave it at the front desk, I will pick it up in a few minutes."

I left her the check, and it was only a few minutes until she picked it up. I told the lady at the front desk I wanted to talk to the lady when she came to get her check. She wasn't as upset about the check being late as she was the way the woman talked to her.

I went to the payroll department where I called the lady outside to talk to her (I never was a person to talk to an employee about their mistakes in front of other employees). I asked her if she thought she needed to apologize to the lady.

She said, "I do and I will call her when I get home. We both will be off work." She did. The next day the employee's wife called me to tell me how she appreciated the phone call from the lady in the payroll department. They became friends and had lunch together a couple times a week.

***

Once I was coming down the river below Memphis. There was a place I should have backed up and flanked. I had it in my head I could steer so I decided I would steer the bend. It didn't work and I had barges all over the river. I called the office and told them I should have flanked, but I didn't.

"Henry, you know you can't steer that bend at this stage of the river with a twenty-barge tow."

"I know it and I just didn't use the better judgment."

He said, "When you get to Greenville, we'll talk about it."

They had me a relief when I got to Greenville. I had my bags when I went in the office. The port captain asked if there anyone else steering the bend.

"Not that I know of," I said. "I just goofed, plain and simple."

He said, "Let me think about it."

I said, "There isn't anything to think about. I either have got a job, or don't."

He said, "Let's go eat."

We went out to the country club to eat. He said, "Henry, I have rode the boat with you at different times and you always used good judgment. You knew when to or not to flank. Why didn't you flank this time when you knew you couldn't steer the bend and out run those dikes? Would you try it again?"

"The river would have to be five higher than it is now. I would steer it," I said.

The man that owned the company came in and sat with us. We went on with our discussion and after a while, he said, "Go on home and catch the boat northbound."

I said, "Take me to the office so I can get my truck."

We went to the office; I put my bags in my truck. He came out and told me to wait a few minutes. It was more than a few minutes. I went into the office. I was in talking to the owner about this and that. He and I were always talking. We talked about everything from picking cotton to what the future of electronics in the pilot-house would be like.

The port captain came in, said, "Get your bag; you are going to Quincy, Illinois, to get on a boat. The captain has his thirty days in and wants off to take care of some business that I forgot about."

I flew to Quincy, got on the boat, came on south, stopped in Cairo, added five more barges (which gave me twenty) and came on south. I was on watch when we got to where I hit ground and broke the boat tow up. You know what? I flanked the bend. I think if I hadn't told him the truth, I would have been out of here. Why? Because he knew I knew better. I know there have been other second chances for me, but this stands out because he sent me north to come south on a boat again with twenty barges. This time, if the river would have been five feet higher, I would have still flanked. There would be no third chance.

21. Locks and Veggies

We were northbound and had just cleared Gallopolis Locks. A couple deckhands were in the pilot-house with me. One said, "I wish you would look at that corn growing out there. If we have to wait on the lock southbound, we will have fresh corn."

I told them to leave that corn alone. We went on into Pittsburgh and when we came back out, we had to wait at Gallopolis Locks. I went to bed and was sound asleep. I could just barely hear somebody calling my name. I got up and walked around the boat where I met two other men who had heard my name. Out on the bank, two of my men stood with a man holding a shotgun. These were not the two men I told not to go out there. I went out to talk to the man with the shotgun. He told me the two men were going to jail. They had two sacks of corn. I asked the man with the shotgun would he take some groceries and let them go. He said, "Maybe."

"What do you want?"

He poured the corn out on the ground, came on the boat, and he got two sacks of groceries. We didn't get the corn.

There were many locks that had good gardens nearby and we would trade groceries for fresh vegetables, but this corn didn't belong to the lock people. The next time we passed, I asked one of my men that went to the cornfield did he want to go get some corn. He said, "I don't even like corn now."

***

At old lock fifty, they always had a good garden and we always got more than we gave. They mostly wanted coffee and sugar. I think the corn was the only time we came up short.

The man that owned the company had got on at lock fifty-one and I let a deckhand drive his car up river. The lock called and wanted to know if we needed any vegetables. The pilot was on watch and didn't know what to tell them because the owner was in the pilot-house. He knew I was up so he called me. I went to the pilot-house and I talked to the lock man. He told me what all he had, then I asked him what he needed. He said three pounds of coffee two bags of sugar. I called the cook and told her what we could get. She told me and I told the lock man. The owner was watching and listening to the whole transaction.

We got up on the lock wall and the lock man came with an old wooden apple box full of vegetables. We gave him what he wanted. The owner hadn't said a word. He went downstairs and I went with him. He looked in the box and told me he wanted to talk. I thought this was it. We went back on the stern, he asked, "Do you think you can get the same trade for me?"

I walked up on the lock wall to talk to the lock man. I said, "Can you fix me up another box for the same trade?"

He said, "It won't be the same thing on a couple items, but I can give a little extra of this and that."

"That will be fine," I told him the owner was on the boat and this was for him. He filled the box over full.

When the owner saw it, he said, "Give them a little extra of what they need. I wish I could make trades like that all time."

When he got off, he took box with him. He called three days later, telling me how good everything was. I was sure glad of that. The pilot had told me he didn't know what to do with the owner on there.

***

There were a number of places where we could trade for fresh vegetables. There were some people that lived just above lock thirteen. They had a little boat and they would come out and we would do a little trading. These people wanted coffee, sugar, and tea. They asked one time did I have a couple cans of hominy.

He said, "I love that stuff and we can't buy it here." I called the cook and asked her did we have a couple spare cans of hominy. We gave him two cans.

There were a couple places on the upper river that did this. You could blow your horn three times and they would come quickly with what they had. One time, this woman came out with a boatload of stuff. She told the cook to get somebody to unload the boat, which was filled with the last of their garden. The cook told me the woman was in her sixties or seventies,

The cook said, "We don't need all that. Can you unload it and give it to a lock or other boats?"

She said her husband had a heart attack while they were working in the garden and he told her to pick what she could and give it to a boat. The next lock we came to, there were some boats waiting on the lock. We gave everything away that the cook didn't want. Waste not, want not.

22. Sixty-Two Years to Sum it Up

Over my boating career, I would get tired of the river. I would get me a job on the Gulf Intracoastal Waterways or the Houston Ship Channel. I would run as mate or deckhand for a change of pace. I quit one time and worked as an engineer on a tug with a 400-horsepower Atlas engine. This was confining, hot, and a lot of work. I knew what I was getting into before I did this because I had done it before.

Once, I went to work in the office for one of the largest boat operators in the world. They sold their inland fleet of boat and barges. I was offered a job in their worldwide operation, but I wanted to stick with the inland waterways. When I left the company, my brother and I got us a boat and went to boat towing on the Gulf Intracoastal Waterways. We made more money than ever, but we didn't like it. Later on, he and I both went back to the river. We never left the river again until we retired. I retired before he did. I had been off about a year when I went to see him. I told him that I missed the boats some.

He said, "Well, if you had a pine knot in your pocket as long as you been riding the boats, then you lay it down, you will miss it."

I had learned three or four other trades that I could turn to, that one man helped me to train for, where I could make as much money and in some cases more than I could on the boats. I did do some of them part time. I liked the boats and I had the nerves to do the job without taking a little white pill. When I retired, I didn't miss the good things. It was bad bridges, locks, bad stretch of river. I was a pressure type of fellow. The more pressure I was under, the better I performed.

My entire boating career, I liked change. I would run with oil boat tows on the canals and rivers, and then I would want to run in the GIWW for a short time. I quit a captain's job on the river and went to decking in the Houston harbor at less than half the money I was making. I quit the boats for short periods of time to do other work connected to boats one way or other. I liked barge line tows on the river best of all.

I always tried to make this a habit. At watch changing time, never turn the controls over to the captain or pilot if I was lining up for a bridge or going in a lock or bad place in the river. If the captain told me to let him have the control, he got them. Also, I would never take the controls if I was coming on watch at one of these places. I learned this when I first went to work in the pilot-house. Something else, I always wanted to know just where I was when I took the controls. When a pilot or captain came on watch, he needed to get the feel of the boat before going into a bad place.

I think I should put this in somewhere, and this as good place as any. I would say 90% of the boat owners I have worked for, that I had personal contact with, have always been up-front with me.

We were on dry dock when the owner showed up that I did not know. I was introduced to him, then I went on my way. He came looking for me. We went to the pilot-house where he said he wanted to talk. By the third word that came out of his mouth, I knew he was lying. He went on trying to give me this snow job. I listened for a while until I finally stopped him and said, "Look, I didn't start running a boat yesterday. Not one word of truth has come out of your mouth since you have been talking." I figured I was fired then and there. He got up and left. He came back late that afternoon, where we met and talked just like nothing ever happened. He knew I knew he was lying without me telling him.

What I have written has taken me close to sixty-two years of putting notes together of my experiences. When it first started out, it was for my children to read, to see how the beans were put on the table. Working on boats was good for me, in part, because there was a lot of pressure, which I enjoyed. The more pressure, the more I enjoyed it. Now it's a different story. I have worked with first class equipment; I have worked on a lot of junk. I won't say working on junk is all bad, because you can learn a lot on how to make do with what you got.

The last company I worked for was a good company. My boss was a man that gave his people the best he could. I stayed with this company longer than I had any other company. On my time off, I would go make a short trip in the gulf intra-coastal canal to keep up-to-date on the canal.

Over the years, I have had a lot of people to ask me why would people ship by barge. The only thing I could tell them it was less expensive. I couldn't give them the exact figures. When I started my book, I did some research between barges, trains, and trucks. I also found the comparison in pollution for each mode of transportation. A recent study conducted by the Texas Transportation Institute compared transport emissions per ton-mile (emissions generated while moving one ton of cargo one mile). Researchers calculated that transport by rail emits 30% more CO2 and transport by truck emits in excess of 900% more CO2, than transport by inland barge. Cost: Barges move one ton of cargo 616 miles per gallon of fuel, a rail car moves the same ton of cargo 478 miles, and a truck only 150 miles. Pollution: In terms of CO2 produced per ton of cargo moved, inland barges have a significant advantage over trains and trucks.

Like I said before, I had some other trades I could go to, besides working on boats and earn good money. I enjoyed working on boats, there was good food and most of all was to have all those days off. The last job I had and retired from we worked thirty days on and thirty days off. The down side was always being away from the family.

When I retired, I had to because of injuries to my neck and back, and the next few years were rough. There were times when I would be paralyzed from the neck down, or the waist down. My main problem was the doctors wouldn't operate, because they said I could be permanently paralyzed with one slip. I was told that in time, I would be paralyzed from the neck down. When this happens, I should then have surgery, because I wouldn't have anything to lose.

Sometimes, I would have to be laid out straight on my back until things began to work. It may take an hour, or several hours. I could usually tell when it was fixing to happen, but not always. If I was driving, I would always have enough notice to stop, and then someone would have to come after me.

There were times when my wife would have to help me dress or take a bath. I just kept doing what my family doctor told me to do for years and I began to get better. I can tell you one thing, for a person that had been doing just about anything they wanted to, then wake up paralyzed from the neck down, your past life will run through your mine in just a short time—good and bad.

I had been off the boat about a year when I called the company about riding from Greenville to St. Louis, and back to Greenville. I had to take one of my sons to help me dress and whatever I needed. We got on at Greenville, and the boat vibration was so bad on my back, that I spent the most of my time on the barges or in bed until we got to Memphis northbound where we had to get off. After this, it never bothered me about going back to the boats until I got a lot better. I came home and started a new life. The hardest job I ever had in my life was doing nothing. I sold all my tools and anything else that required the use of my back and neck. Almost thirty years later my neck will lock up sometimes and in time it will pass.

This is part of my boating career in print.

Glossary

Life on the river has its own language. I'll do my best to explain riverboat terminology.

For starters:

Driving a bridge- When you are going to drive a bridge, you get lined up for the bridge, push the throttles full ahead and hope for the best.

Stern - back of the boat.

Bow -front of the boat.

Starboard - right.

Port - left.

A mate - the twelve-to-six watch in the canal.

A pilot- what he's called on the river.

A single screw - a boat with one propeller.

A twin screw - a boat with two propellers.

A triple screw- a boat with three propellers.

Flank - that for some reason, or another, you can't steer around bend south-bound because the river channel isn't wide enough. Your boat tow can get into a slide sideways. The boat will slide in the river bank, or on whatever is in the bend. You have to back up so that the boat tow is below the current's speed. You put the head of the boat tow close to the shore and your stern (back) is in the current, where the current will come down between boat tow and river bank. You move a head keeping the head of boat tow from hitting the river bank. Anytime the channel is not wide enough to steer, you back up and *flank*. What you're doing is floating around the bend, keeping your boat tow in shape to come full ahead when the time is right. This can be above bridges, locks, docks when south-bound. It's very easy to get the boat tow into slide, when you don't need it.

Made in the USA
Monee, IL
09 September 2019